PERFECT
PHRASES
for
SCHOOL
ADMINISTRATORS

D1593377

PERFECT PHRASES

for

SCHOOL
ADMINISTRATORS

**Hundreds of Ready-to-Use Phrases for
Evaluations, Meetings, Contract Negotiations,
Grievances, and Correspondence**

Christine Canning Wilson

New York   Chicago   San Francisco   Lisbon   London   Madrid   Mexico City
Milan   New Delhi   San Juan   Seoul   Singapore   Sydney   Toronto

The McGraw·Hill Companies

Library of Congress Cataloging-in-Publication Data

Wilson, Christine Canning.
    Perfect phrases for school administrators : hundreds of ready-to-use phrases for evaluations, meetings, contract negotiations, grievances, and correspondences / Christine Canning Wilson.
        p.   cm.
    ISBN 0-07-163205-0
    1. Communication in education.   2. Schools—Records and correspondence. I. Title.

    LB1033.5.W553   2009
    371.2′011—dc22   2009040436

1 2 3 4 5 6 7 8 9 10 11 12 13 14 15 16 17 18 19 20 21 22   FGR/FGR   0 9

ISBN   978-0-07-163205-8
MHID   0-07-163205-0

To my late husband, Douglas Wilson, and my beautiful children,
Katherine and Alexander Wilson

To my parents, Kathleen and John Canning, the best teachers, mentors,
and administrators I know

To my brothers, John and Greg, and my sisters,
Kathleen and Maria

And to my best friends, Dr. Christine Coombe, Dr. Lisa Barlow,
Dr. Leah Bornstein, Dr. Linda Day, Lucille Fox, Elaine Plumb,
Mike Galliher, Ibrahim Ali, and Katey-Archey Kerwood

Contents

Contents

Contents

Preface

This book and its sister companion, *Perfect Phrases for Classroom Teachers*, should be the staple of every teacher and administrator training program. School districts should set aside professional-development funds to make sure that teachers and administrators learn the laws, follow the solid recommendations, and put the suggestions for sound practices into action. Often bad practices are passed down through old-boy networks that try to maintain archaic practices in a changed society. Today's administrators must be able to face the challenges facing them in a society that openly litigates and subjects them to new regulations and policies on a regular basis. As a successful whistle-blower on a public school district that violated the health, welfare, and safety of children, I know what is happening from the inside and have spoken up against the injustices found in public education. Many cover ups, scandals, and problems faced by districts are a result of malpractice. This book was written to educate administrators and educators on the laws, practices, and recommendations needed to protect their positions and the reputation of their school within the district. No longer can administrators close a blind eye, bully, or use intimidating practices because we live in a more transparent and global society. I wrote this book to help modern administrators learn how to take proactive measures to protect the children entrusted into their care and to better serve the district that employs them to take managerial charge of faculty, curriculum, policy, and procedures.

This book should serve as the practical, everyday guide for educators and administrators everywhere who want to be more effective, forward thinking, and on the cutting edge of their professional practice. May the examples cited in this book along with the phrases help you to become an even greater influence in the educational upbringing of all you come in contact with during your prosperous career.

Acknowledgments

I would like to acknowledge my professional colleagues Jodi Klein, Deb Zacarian, David Valade, Graciela Trilla, Betsy Tregar, Jude Travers, Helen Soranzo, Vula Roumis, Meg Palladino, Jennifer O'Brien, Kara Mitchell, Paula Merchant, Kathy Lobo, Kellie Jones, Sara Hamerla, Melanie Grietzer, Diane Epstein, Joanne Fridley, Linda Foley-Vinay, Ann Feldman, Boni Ester Enquist, Robin Dowling Grant, Anne Dolan, Suzanne Coffin, Nancy Cloud, Lynn Bonesteel, Beth Benedict, Margaret Adams, Rob Vitello, Marnie Reed, Paul Abraham, Winifred Wood, and the members of MATSOL. I would like to thank my colleagues of Northern New England TESOL and their great leader, Beth Evans. Thanks to the great conference team that awarded me a position as the local chairperson for TESOL International, especially Melissa Latham, Diane Carter, Leslie Barrett, Lisa Dyson, and our local team leaders, whose invaluable help will never be forgotten.

Thanks also to the clients and educational consultants of New England Global Network LLC, in western Massachusetts, and to the Lanesborough School District and its miracle worker, Elizabeth Nichols. Thanks to the graduates of the class of 1987 of Saint Joseph's High School and to my faux mother-in-law, Fran Tierney.

Thanks to those I have worked with in the MTA, NEA, DOD, DOT, Peace Corps, MCCC, the foreign-language department at Wilbraham High School in Ludlow, Massachusetts, and at West Virginia University, under the direction of Dr. Robert Elkins, Dr. Seyneave, Dr. Shlunk, Dr. Powers, and Dr. Fakri. A great thanks to my friends and supporters in the United Educators of Pittsfield, Massachusetts, as well as to the MCCC's Joe Rizzo, the BCC's Ellen Shanahan, and, of course, the MTA's Miles Stern.

Thanks to my editor, Kathryn Kiel, and the great team under the direction of Craig Bolt at McGraw-Hill. And I mustn't forget to thank my favorite lawyers, Michael Hinkley, Steve Pagnotta, and Phil Grandchamp, from the educational law firm Donovan and O'Connor, in North Adams, Massachusetts.

Thank you to my support colleagues working for the United Arab Emirates Presidential Court; the governments in Central Asia, North Africa, the Middle East, Arabian Gulf, and former Russian Republics; the Higher Colleges of Technology, United Arab Emirates; United Arab Emirates University and UGRU; the British Council, TESOL Arabia, the U.S. Department of State; and public affairs offices in U.S. embassies in Dushanbe, Tunis, Kiev, Abu Dhabi, Bahrain, Qatar, Kuwait, Kyrgyzstan; with special thanks to Andrea Schindler, Lisa Harshbarger, Alonya, Fatema Hashem, Sami Saieed, Joe Parris, Marita Lawson, Scott Waldo, Jackie McKennan, Mehkrimisso Pirmatova, Julia Walters, and all the others who make it happen for teachers around the world.

A special thanks to the top professionals I have ever been blessed to know: Patricia Sanchez, Pam Appel, Margaret and Quinlan Rodriguez, Lil Quinn, Judy Fairweather, Anthony Antil, Justin Miaa, Paul Perry, Gordy Roberts, Carol Chanen, Don Coudert, Steve Antil, Nancy Hubley, Cecelia Kawar, Lily Ford, Sue Powell, Joanne Zoller Wagner and Rebbie McIntyre, Dara Shaw, Becky Loomis, Ann Marie Ziadie, Maryanne Harrar, MaryJo and Tonya, Marlys Berg, Lisa Pularo-Spazioso, Marylou Galliher, Jill and Chris LaBeau, Elizabeth Nichols, Sue Tourigney, Sue Chapman, Jane Shiya, Ward Johnson, Jenn Schnopp, Marion Gennette, Michelle Murphy, Judy Williamson, Carol Daily, Lisa Messina, Mrs. Leonard, Anna Mello, Bernadette McMahon, Sharon Kokoefer, Prudence Barton, Kevin Dowling, Ellen Bosche, Marie Russell, Kirsten Hoffstedt, Donna Paglier, John Lunt, Chris White, Chris Supple, Amanda Defer, Mary Maroon, Mary Monette, Dawn Hertzberg, Suzanne Harrison, Joyce Culverwell, Judy Williamson, Marlee

Terry, Molly Kirk, Nancy Giftos, Anita Plouffe, Andrea Schindler, Lisa Dafarra Gold, Nancy Giftos, Anita Plouffe, and Denise Withers.

Dr. Suliman Al-Batel, Dr. Tayeb Kamali, Steve Allison, Norm Breault, Casey Malarcher, Stephen Kochuba, Phil Quirke, Paul Mayes, Greg Bubniak, Mark Beatty, Greg Saleh, Ed Carlstedt, Elliott Dreger, Barbara Miller; Armando D'Silva, Sandra Fox, Sandra Smith, Nedra White; Massachusetts State Office of Minority and Women Business Assistance (SOMWBA); the superb female leaders who run the successful Massachusetts Affirmative Market Program: Maria Gonzalez, Donna Fleser, and Gladymar Parziale; Cambridge University's CELTA and DELTA Program; and, of course, Tim Smith, Liz Howell, Nicolette Marsden, Lynn Nicks McCaleb, Richard Monterosso, and Elspeth Cavalcanti. A special spot of recognition to the Educational Faculty of Massachusetts College of Liberal Arts, especially Dr. Roselle Chartock and Dr. Ellen Barber, as well as the University of Massachusetts at Amherst's Graduate Education ERPA Doctoral Program under the direction of Dr. Joe Berger and my mentor, Dr. Sangeeta Kamat.

Introduction

Thank you for investing in this valuable resource book for school administrators. In time, it may come to be your bible of reference on various issues that affect schools and school districts. This book will first explain the concepts in education and legalities of education and then offer you chapters of perfect phrases to use in your work.

Understanding Leadership and Leadership Choices

First let us examine what it means to be an educational leader. It is important to remember that as a leader, you are choosing a lonely path. Often you are like a fish in a fishbowl, watched by different parties and judged according to how your actions meet their expectations. If you intend to be a leader in education, you have to be thick-skinned. You have to understand that school leadership is not personal, but rather business. If you can approach it from this angle, there is a great chance you will be a top-notch educational leader.

   Training for school administrators varies from state to state. And although educational leaders go through training and practicum, the fact remains that most people train near their home areas, so that the same errors, practices, and methods are reintroduced to the fresh blood that should be entering the system. So quite often real improvement in education never happens. To empower yourself as an educational leader, it is important that you do the following:

- Recognize your own strengths and weaknesses.
- Investigate matters without bias.
- Keep information confidential.
- Know your rights and those of your employees.
- Comment when necessary and remain tight-lipped when possible.
- Live by example.
- Don't undercut your staff.
- Keep your ego intact.
- Understand that there is more than one way to do something.
- Bring out the best in your faculty and staff.
- Know what is going on at all times by being the pulse of your school.
- Write objective evaluations.
- Avoid using anonymous people and "what if" situations to control others.
- Avoid miscommunication or lying.
- Know how to delegate.
- Keep a positive outlook and attitude.
- Be seen at events.
- Promote others in your school by highlighting them in papers.
- Counsel faculty on the best classroom practices.
- Be able to fight the fight when budget battles arise.
- Like learning and love students.
- Foster growth and see people's potential.

It has long been suggested that leadership involves power by influence and management involves power by position, and if this is the case, we must accept that schools will consist of both leaders and managers. Sometimes members of committees, administrations, and faculty can do more harm than good in influencing morale in a school. It is often the case that when people aren't at their best, they seldom make the best decisions. You should avoid the following mistakes of poor educational leaders:

- Misrepresenting situations
- Misallocating funding
- Covering up incidents that should be reported
- Causing dissent and division among faculty
- Risking grievance or union problems by breaking collective bargaining agreements
- Harassing individual teachers
- Bullying faculty members
- Threatening people's job security to promote your own interests
- Showing signs of disregard or disrespect toward colleagues
- Retaliating against those who speak out against you
- Blackballing teachers from employment in other districts
- Not following local, state, and federal laws
- Not responding to faculty, parent, or community e-mails
- Engaging in controlling and/or deviant behavior
- Undermining or targeting certain individuals
- Playing favorites
- Manipulating situations
- Humiliating or threatening individuals
- Pitting faculty members against one another for personal gain
- Being caught up in scandals
- Bringing lawsuits upon the district based on poor decisions
- Avoiding tackling issues
- Passing the buck and not assuming responsibility
- Blaming others for your own inaccuracies

- Envying other educational administrators or faculty
- Playing games
- Not getting involved where you should be involved

As we know, making choices and decisions is critical to a working school environment. Understanding the purpose, identity, and responsibilities of your role in the school community is essential. Educational leaders have to ask themselves the following questions about a decision:

- Is what I am doing ethical?
- Is it in the best interests of the children I serve?
- How will it affect the community?
- How will I involve teachers?
- What are the pros and cons?
- Will it pass a school committee or the board of education for approval?
- Is it transparent for all to see?
- If it is taken to court, can we win?
- If something goes wrong, who will be held responsible and why?
- Does it follow district policy?
- Is it legal?
- Does it protect the health, welfare, and safety of children?
- What will the faculty's overall reaction be?
- As the educational administrator, can I live with the decision I've made?
- What will be the fallout if this situation is not handled properly?
- Who will come out of the woodwork, and what documents or evidence might they have that would further incriminate our handling of the situation?
- Can a simple apology solve a problem before it escalates?

During your educational tenure, you need to be able to adapt. As an educator it is your job to convey a sense of purpose so as to foster development. This may mean that as an educational leader you grow in the areas of social and cultural competence. This may also mean you have to become the salmon that swims against the river's current, with the risk of being eaten by the bear at the end of the journey. Only time will tell, based on the leadership choices you make. Some will roll with the punches, others will sweep issues under the carpet, many will boldly take the bull by the horns, and some will fossilize like a dinosaur until retirement. Along the way you will encounter dissatisfied employees, students of all learning abilities, both involved and uninvolved parents, members of the community, and school boards, all of whom will believe that you are there to serve their needs.

In other words, your legacy as an educational leader will be determined by the people you help, as well as by the mistakes you make. To become an educational leader you must be open to new ideas, fair to all people, and not tempted to retaliate from the secured power of your administrative position against those who question your motives. Instead of getting angry, you may want to consider what they are saying. Remember, there are always two sides to an issue. You will learn to work with labor unions, to improve your negotiation skills, to understand compromise, and to put your foot down based on well-informed and sound judgments.

It is an educational administrator's duty to support social justice and to promote equal educational opportunities for students. You will make choices in curriculum and instruction that impact students' formal years of learning. You will need to decide the best course for presenting information to young learners and methods for managing scores of people from different walks of life. The most important thing you should remember is that you will be held accountable for your actions. Your decisions will be impacted not only by your judgment, but by budgetary constraints, state and federal laws, government policies, children, parents, committees, community groups, and of course, taxpayers! As a leader you need to bring people and programs together by linking information between sectors. This means you will need to have a knowledge base and an ability to move toward defining performance in all areas of your school. This may be done through hiring people with proper teaching qualifications, understanding the roles of teachers and other administrators, fostering both student and professional autonomy, and working with pedagogy and curriculum while meeting leadership demands and needs. As an educational leader you will need to examine what motivating factors, approaches to change, and actions will help you make the best decisions in the interests of children.

Your primary focus will be on maintaining consistency in the workplace, improving conditions for learning, and balancing your personal life with your professional life. As an educational leader or administrator, you will take on new roles and responsibilities while facing challenges and current realities. As a leader you must motivate and inspire others to look at major trends and issues to best serve the student population.

Chapter 1

An Overview of School Law and Discipline

It is essential that all educational leaders in your school be versed in your local, state, and federal laws. Nowadays it isn't just parents taking school districts to court, but rather teachers and others involved in the educational process based on the abuses they see in the system. Educational administrators who scold faculty for reporting incidents or claim that unnecessary referral slips are being written pose a great danger to the learning environment. Heroic parties such as the ACLU (www.aclu.org), educational advocacy groups (www.nea.org), and educational experts (www.negn.org) are working to educate people on their rights.

One of the best advocates for education is the United States federal government. Every educational administrator or leader should regularly request by mail or download current federal government publications related to education from its websites.

For example, the U.S. Constitution requires that all students be given equal educational opportunity regardless of their race, ethnic background, religion, or sex, yet every year cases are brought to the courts or complaints made to the state because educational administrators disregard the simple basics. An administrator or teacher cannot discriminate against a student based on reasons such as economic status, citizenship, or language ability. Even students who are in this country illegally or who are homeless have the right to go to public school and be educated. Districts and administrators can't deny an education to an undocumented child. The learner, while living in this country, is entitled to an education. Other countries have very similar laws, and the rules for the country's ministry of education should be followed.

While students have a right to an education, they can be denied access to a school for some reasons. One of the most common given by educational administrators is if the child doesn't behave in a suitable manner. In these cases, students can receive home tutors or be sent to other facilities to continue their education, especially if they prove to be a threat to other learners. Parents often refuse to believe that school districts have a right to dictate behavior policies. Within the framework of educational laws written at the state, federal, and local levels, districts do have the power to put into place policies that protect the learning environment. Such policies are necessary because schools are not babysitting services; they are institutions of learning.

And much to people's dismay, there is no uniformity regarding which students are allowed to stay in their schools and which are required to go for any particular behaviors. What may be acceptable in one district may not be in another district less than a mile away. For example, some school administrators claim that they would rather have an in-house policy for dealing with bullying, as opposed to a model based on the national zero-tolerance policy used by other districts. Parents who argue, "If my child attended a different school he wouldn't have had this consequence" are probably correct. However, their child doesn't attend that school. Instead, the child attends your school and is subject to your school district's policies.

As an educational leader, you know that school systems have formal policies and rules covering student discipline, referred to as student codes of conduct. A student code of conduct is usually found in a student handbook that students and parents should be required to sign. By saving and documenting the parents' signatures, you have proof that the guardians acknowledge that they understand what is expected of their children while attending school. The school's handbook should specify formal policies and define the nature and severity of student offenses. It should indicate the alternatives of punishment available and designate the person responsible for enforcing each rule and implementing each procedure. For example, the policy book might state that only the assistant principal can suspend a student, and that a teacher can only file a recommendation to suspend a student for just cause, such as insubordination. I would recommend that as an administrator, fairness should be the basis for every decision made. This advice is for your own protection. It is important that you be familiar with school law and record information very carefully to avoid litigation. This section discusses how to document issues related to school law and discipline.

Corporal Punishment

In most states, courts have ruled that students have the right to freedom from bodily restraint under the Fourteenth Amendment of the U.S. Constitution. Unfortunately, media reports have shown that the Fourteenth Amendment is not upheld in every state! In a recent article, one public school boasted, "pass the state boards or get the board!" In Florida, this statement is acceptable, but in other states it would legally be considered child abuse. This is a clear and unfortunate example of our country's lack of uniformity on the issue of corporal punishment. In states where corporal punishment has been permitted, some school districts and their administrators have been sued for corporal punishments in cases that have led to broken bones and other injuries. Much to many educational leaders' disbelief, courts have held that the Eighth Amendment (the amendment that forbids "cruel and unusual punishment") applies only in a criminal context, and not in student discipline proceedings. United States courts have, however, recognized the right of students to be informed of prohibited behaviors. Courts have further afforded pupils certain procedural safeguards prior to the imposition of corporal punishment. So, then, what are the ramifications of these court mandates for the administrator?

- First, they suggest that parents cannot argue that requiring a student to copy from the dictionary, confiscating a cell phone, or throwing out gum are cruel and unusual punishments.
- They also imply that parents or guardians can argue that excessive force was used on their child. This opens up the gates for scrutiny and litigation and may make school administrators think twice before placing a hand on a child entrusted to their care.

Hitting children is nothing new in schools. Around the world, children are harshly disciplined daily. I have worked in a state that forbids teachers to touch students with any physical force, but that doesn't mean teachers haven't done it. If a teacher touches a student, even in some states that allow corporal punishment, the teacher can be in clear violation of the law and can face assault charges. In some cases, where the laws of corporal punishment are followed haphazardly, teachers can still be in violation if they grab, tug, hit, or have any physical contact with a student as a form of discipline.

The federal government has no comprehensive policy on this issue. It is up to each state to decide upon the use of corporal punishment in schools. Thus any legal justification for using corporal punishment is found in state statutes. For example, in the Commonwealth of Massachusetts corporal punishment is prohibited, but in other states, such as Florida, it is permitted. As an administrator, you will find that federal and state courts have consistently upheld its reasonable use where the state allows it, but not in the twenty or more states that ban its practice. If you want to know your state's current position on corporal punishment, this information is available online at http://school.family education.com/classroom-discipline/resource/38377.html.

The United States Supreme Court has further stated that if corporal punishment is allowed, there are nine general guidelines on what constitutes "reasonable" physical contact. If your school permits corporal punishment, you can get information on policies and interpretation for corporal punishment by state online at www.corpun.com/usscr2a.htm. However, remember that as an administrator you should not rely on websites to set policy, but you should be familiar with your state's laws as well as U.S. and state supreme court and lower court decisions for clarification. For example, according to the U.S. Supreme Court, any corporal punishment of students must meet the following nine requirements:

- It must be allowed by state statute (either directly or by inference).
- It must be appropriate for the offense. For example, forgetting a pencil for class would not justify hitting a seven-year old with a paddle repeatedly on the buttocks.
- It must be implemented consistently with state statutory requirements.
- It must be used as a method of correction. This means that the teacher can't just hit a child out of anger on the spur of the moment.
- It must involve use of an appropriate instrument. For example, teachers or administrators can't use devices that burn the skin like cigarettes or cattle prods. The use of rulers on the knuckles of a child, although used in the schools when I was a child, most likely could not be justified in a court of law today.
- It must not be cruel or excessive. This is very interpretive, so school administrators should be very careful, because what is acceptable to you may not be to an outsider.

- It must not involve anger or malice.
- It must not leave permanent or lasting injuries, such as battered and bloody knuckles resulting from a child's fingers being hit with a ruler.
- It must suit the age, gender, and physical condition of the child. Before administering corporal punishment, school administrators should consider whether children have any special needs.

The U.S. Supreme Court has also ruled that four procedural guidelines should be followed:

1. Students must be warned in advance of the specific kinds of behavior that could result in their being corporally punished. This means a teacher can't just yank a child in front of the room and start beating the student for something he or she has done without prior warning that the behavior could result in corporal punishment.
2. The act of corporal punishment **is not to be the first line of punishment**. The student should be given some type of verbal or written reprimand before any physical contact takes place.
3. If corporal punishment is administered to a student, a second school official must be present to witness the act. As many of us know, that isn't always practiced and can be grounds for legal action.
4. The parents of a punished student must be furnished on request with a written statement about the act, including reasons for it and the names of the witnesses.

Rules on corporal punishment have improved over the past twenty years, but until more parents and students speak up, out, and against the practice, it will continue to flourish.

In private and parochial schools, corporal punishment statutes vary by state.

Search and Seizure

Search and seizure issues have always been of great interest to me. My father was the principal of a district that was the test case on this issue in the Commonwealth of Massachusetts when I was a child. As the Fourth Amendment to the U.S. Constitution provides the right of the people to be "secure in their persons, houses, papers, and effects, against unreasonable searches and seizures," it requires that police and authorities follow legal procedures before they may search and seize the property belonging to a citizen. The reason my father and his district won the case that is now taught in educational law classes is because he and his colleagues had written into the district policies and handbook that the lockers were the property of the school. Therefore, as the educational administrator, he had the right to search a locker, since the school "owned" the locker and the locker was not the property of the student. Although the courts have not extended this policy to school police officers, school administrators can search school lockers without warrants, provided that their policy is clearly written in the school handbook for all to see. Search and seizure of backpacks and persons, unlike lockers, is still not permissible, as they are not owned by districts, and can be a Fourth Amendment violation [*New Jersey v. T.L.O.*, 469 U.S. 325 (1985)].

Smoking, Drugs, and Alcohol

Every school needs to address the issues of smoking, drugs, and alcohol on school premises. Sometimes teachers who are smokers can be seen outside of a school building with cigarettes alongside students. Some schools overlook this, and others have strict penalties. Some schools neglect to address the issue, instead choosing to focus on issues that they feel are of more relevance. However, schools must ban smoking by students because the minimum smoking age in the United States is eighteen. If students are eighteen, they can smoke legally, but they cannot smoke on school grounds. In most states schools are considered public buildings, and smoking would be in violation of public health laws.

In a recent deposition, an administrator stupidly claimed that although he didn't smoke, he didn't prevent students from smoking cigarettes on the curb outside the back doors of the school because he felt it prevented them from going off into the woods to smoke pot. As an educational administrator, you don't have the authority to make those types of decisions. Instead, you must work within the guidelines of state and local laws.

On a similar but related issue, states have different laws and views on drugs. Some states are more strict than others. Massachusetts has a law that requires a mandatory sentence of two and a half years in prison for selling drugs within a school zone. As the administrator, you need to know what your state regulations are regarding drug dealing, use, and possession. It is also important to know the law regarding the sale of prescription drugs and to formulate a policy compliant with that law. It is quite common for students to sell their medications for extra cash. You may also want to consider what the school policy is if a student takes a drug off campus—especially if the drug's effect on the child's behavior impacts the campus itself when the student returns to school. As an administrator, you may want to have a policy on marijuana use. Some schools have drug tests performed by nurses. Parents have sued administrators, arguing that a school district has no right to take a student's DNA. As an administrator, you must check your state laws and work with legal experts to write policies that comply with state mandates, especially if your district insists on random drug testing. Recently, the legality of random drug testing of athletes has been challenged by the American Civil Liberties Union. The ACLU claimed in a Tennessee case that "it has proven to be ineffective in deterring drug use and is opposed by leading experts in adolescent health, including the American Academy of Pediatrics, the National Education Association, the Association of Addiction Professionals, and the National Association of Social Workers." So, as an educational administrator, before you start testing students' urine or blood, you may want to consult the district's attorney.

The public seems to be bombarded daily with stories of cases involving students and substance use. A famous case involved parents who were held liable by authorities for serving alcohol to students at a non-school-sanctioned party. Another case years ago involved a student putting laxatives into brownies, affecting other children's bowel movements; although school officials knew about the incident, they didn't take action until after the parents brought charges. Back then, lacing foods or pouring substances into drinks was frowned upon, but today it can be a criminal offense. Often students aren't harming other students, but rather the learner causes self-injury with substance use. A common problem schools have faced is students putting alcohol in soda bottles and drinking during the school day. Regardless of your position on student drinking, the fact remains that the legal drinking age in the United States is twenty-one. Therefore, it is illegal for persons under the age of twenty-one to drink alcoholic beverages on school grounds or at any school event.

Self-inflicted wounds with pens, pencils, and razors are also becoming more commonplace, as is sniffing glue and other inhalants. These issues must also be addressed in student handbooks. Recently, the Bronx police raided a fifth grade drug operation in an elementary school, so the rules should be written to apply to all students of all ages. Handbooks should be written to release schools from liabilities that cannot be foreseen, but now with local press coverage, it is hard to say that anything can't be foreseen. In the 1980s, a student was sliced in half after "elevator surfing"—now schools implement elevator safety tips in their handbooks. With the growth of MySpace, Facebook, cellular coverage, podcasts, and YouTube, schools have had to write policies to protect themselves against students who wear school sports uniforms while posing with alcohol in posted pictures that can represent the image of the school on the Internet.

Handbooks should also be written in this regard for teachers, as some have been known to drink on school grounds, drink with students, or promote alcohol in other inappropriate ways. I strongly advise that administrators not hold meetings other than on school grounds. In a recent deposition against a school district, it was pointed out that faculty meetings were "held over drinks" in a barlike atmosphere. This is very damaging for the school district, as the actions serve as an improper model of behavior on the part of both teachers and administrators.

Teachers and administrators have a responsibility to provide a safe environment for the students that is conducive to learning. Thus, school districts must work in compliance with their local laws to write individual policies to state their position on the use, sale, or possession of tobacco, alcohol, or drugs on school property. If no policies are put into place or action, teachers, administrators, students, or parents can contact their state public health department and file a complaint.

Freedom of Speech in Schools

How many times as an educator have you heard a student tell a teacher or other adult, "You can't tell me what I can or can't say because you are not my mother!" This is both true and untrue in a school setting. It is true that the First Amendment guarantees citizens' rights to free expression and free association. This means that the government does not have the right to prevent us from saying and writing what we like. As citizens, we can form clubs and organizations and take part in demonstrations and rallies. But that does not give a person the right to yell "fire" in a crowded theater or to communicate in other ways that endanger the public. Second, in fact, while children are in school, the teacher or administrator according to law does function in the role of their parent, under the concept of in loco parentis.

Many teachers and educational leaders are deeply confused about what a student may and may not say. As we know, the Supreme Court has held that it is a violation of the First Amendment for the government to make citizens say something they don't want to say. In one case, a student argued that he was given detention for not pledging allegiance. It was determined that the student was correct in claiming that he had the right to remain silently seated during the Pledge of Allegiance. The teacher sent him to the office for not standing up to pledge under the charge of insubordination. The vice principal issued a detention slip to the student, who turned a copy over to a law firm that was suing the district on behalf of another plaintiff for similar violations. The lack of knowledge of the law by the educational administrator was another nail in the coffin for the school district. If you are unsure about students' free speech rights, school districts consider the major decision on this topic to be *Tinker v. Des Moines Independent Community School District.* This Supreme Court decision held that students in public schools do not leave their First Amendment rights at the "schoolhouse gate." This means that students can express their opinions orally and in writing, in leaflets or on buttons, armbands, or T-shirts. According to the courts, it is all legal as long as the student's speech doesn't "materially and substantially" disrupt classes or other school activities and is not incorporated into documents published by the school.

But as you know, there are modifications that have come along since the *Tinker* case. For example, as an administrator or teacher you can modify speech in a public school when it interferes with the normal functioning of the learning environment, such as when students hold a protest in the cafeteria and block free access points to it. On a similar note, you can probably stop students from using vulgar or indecent language, but be aware that students may argue that even the FCC has approved the "*f* word" in certain contexts. For example, English teachers are known to teach about it as it relates to British literature because it once stood for Fornication Under Consent of the King.

Keep in mind as a school administrator that the ACLU is quick to point out that you "may not censor only one side of a controversy." For example, if your school presents an article regarding the funding of abstinence education, both sides of the issue must be given equal treatment. Such things do not hold true in private and parochial schools, as they are not held to the same standards due to their lack of funding or ownership by the U.S. federal government. Thus, at a Catholic school, a teacher who suggests to a child that the use of condoms is best to prevent STDs may legally be fired, as this statement may violate the principles of that particular institution's philosophy.

As an administrator, you may be surprised at what students feel they have the right to say, and with that in mind, it is good to be aware of the 1998 Supreme Court decision of *Hazelwood School District v. Kuhlmeier*. Here it was determined that public school administrators can censor student speech in official school publications or activities if the officials think students are saying something "inappropriate" or "harmful," despite if its use is not vulgar or does not cause disruption. Some states, such as the Commonwealth of Massachusetts, have high school free expression laws that give students greater rights of free speech. So it is important that you check with your board of education to find out whether your state has such laws on its books.

Dress Code

Depending on your state's laws, be aware as an administrator that schools may be able to control what students wear, and schools may be able to create hair codes. For the most part, students can wear their hair in any fashion, as long as it is not a safety hazard as defined by the school. For example, in a vocational school, students in a welding or machine shop may be required to wear steel toe boots and have their hair tied back while using equipment. Much to student dismay, school districts for the most part can create dress codes and enforce them, especially if the students' choice of clothing disrupts the learning environment. However, what is offensive to one person may be acceptable to another. Therefore, it is recommended that illustrations of acceptable clothing be drawn along with the wording for clear interpretation in the handbook.

I have heard female students who have been asked not to wear tube tops that reveal their stomachs, upper arms, and shoulders argue that it is unfair, since boys can be bare-chested in public. This is why nonsexist language and policies need to be written. On a similar note, some boys like to wear pants that reveal their underwear, and this may be considered equally offensive, as undergarments should not be seen in public schools. It is highly recommended to have a clear dress code policy, and it is equally important that the code be consistently enforced, or it could become a great source of tension!

Keep in mind that the reality of dress codes can be an interpretive nightmare. For every rule an administrator creates, there is a student to challenge it. For example, students rebel by cutting holes into clothing to reveal skin or begin to wear clothing so tight that it appears to be body painted. One thing that most schools agree with when it comes to dress code is banning gang-related clothing and clothing that might prove dangerous, such as baggy sweats or pants that can conceal weapons. At one school where I taught, the administrators banned all bandanas and related headgear. As any educator would imagine, students then brought into question why some girls could wear headbands, but they couldn't wear bandanas! This was resolved by clarifying that hair accessories were acceptable only if worn vertically or horizontally and specifying the types of material that could compose them. Another arguable piece of clothing that has been banned by schools is "sex bracelets." These accessories indicate how many boys girls have been with sexually using different colored bands like bracelets on their wrists. The dress code is a never-ending battle, but it is one that should be carefully addressed in school handbooks.

Cyber Threats and Bullying

While new technology continues to enrich learning experiences, there are some troubling new ways it's being used to threaten kids in American school districts. Hazing was once an issue, and it still is in certain schools, but now the trend in bullying is anonymous blogging. Blogging websites can be used to suggest, damage, libel, and slander a pupil's reputation. One common bullying technique is to engage others to share their top ten list of negative statements about a person via electronic media and computers.

Cyber bullying is the term used to describe the different ways adults and kids may use the Internet to cause harm. Many students choose to text or e-mail threats and horrible statements to unnerve their classmates. The cyber world often enters the school world when students begin a series of harassing incidents that appear isolated but are not. Harassment is understood to be unwanted and repeated attention, but students often think it is a rite of passage. As cyber laws and harassment laws develop based on cases that arise, the law is predicted to change, especially in the next decade. It is important that a district work closely with attorneys to write policies that reflect individual state laws on a yearly basis. This section of the book offers administrators concepts that should be incorporated into school handbooks, policies, and procedures to protect students from other students, parents, teachers, staff, third parties, or administrators who may engage in such activity.

In your handbook you might want to consider a threat to be communication that insults, threatens, or uses lewd pictures or language that is sent using electronic media, is posted for public consumption, or impedes the learning environment. In a recent deposition, a principal discussed how with the use of cell phones, girls had cyber bullied and threatened other girls at school. This led to fistfights and to the ruination of a teacher's reputation. It was implied that the teacher did not properly handle the situation, and moreover, the school had no substantial policy to cover it, which allowed it to escalate further. If the parents of the beaten girls took the case to court, the school would most likely be found liable.

Your school's handbook should clearly state a zero-tolerance policy and clarify the forms of harassment. For example, if a group of girls shout at an overweight student, "Hey, cow," does the district consider that harassment or a one-time form of communication? What if the school ignores the situation, and the next day this is repeated, but this time the group of girls put pictures of cows all over the victim's locker. Then, as the child walks down the hall, students begin to make cow sounds singling her out. At what point does it constitute harassment? Your handbook needs to address a no-tolerance policy; a single or multiple communication policy; or an unwanted increase in communication policy. But what if the same girls go on the Internet and begin signing the child up for websites that encourage weight loss or post her picture on websites like uglypeople.com? As an educational administrator, you should consider a clause that discourages the use of third parties as a form of harassment, especially since companies sell addresses to other similar businesses.

What if the whole situation goes a step further? This time the students take pictures of the victim changing for gym class and send it to other students followed by pictures of bent fingers in up-close shots to insinuate that it is her buttocks. Later that day, the girl begins to be harassed by boys. Perhaps that night she overdoses on sleeping pills and commits suicide. Are you culpable? Has your school implemented a policy with respect to these things? Did your lack of policy or enforcement lead to the girl's suicide or state of mind? These are real issues that educational administrators have to deal with on a daily basis.

As an administrator, your student handbooks and policies should be written to address issues that can be expected to arise. In general, a handbook should address things that administrators and teachers know that students are capable of doing. For example, writing e-mails and sending candy grams to a student that appear to be from another student, using a false persona, can lead to upset. Many students pose as other students to intimidate their victims, or they register students for clubs that might embarrass the victim.

Hollywood films have cashed in on these very common problems in schools. In one film plot, students make false reports using another student's name, and the result is the humiliation of the victim. Another common plot in school-related films centers around students repeating rumors that are known or suspected to be false, especially those with sexual connotations.

Another issue school districts and their handbooks need to address is the sharing or stealing of other students' computer passwords. It is not unheard of for pupils to break into each other's e-mail accounts and send materials out in others' names, and such incidents have been known to involve local authorities. Some have been known to hack into computer systems and demonstrate malicious intent by using technology to damage others. Some have played with school attendance or grade records, and others have sent viruses, shutting down networks. All districts should be able to agree that this is not acceptable and should create written policies against these practices. When I first became aware of this, in the early 1990s, school districts wanted to find the student hacker to offer him or her a job if the child could crack the codes, but today's administrator wants to apprehend the pupil and press charges for violating laws.

The school should also consider writing policies regarding outside events that could affect school time. For example, what if a boy who has been "dumped" by his girlfriend posts her cell phone number, locker number, bus route, and/or address on a teen chat site? As a result a third party begins to stalk her, and she finds notes and other objects in her locker. This is unwanted and threatening attention, and it is not acceptable, but in this case it becomes increasingly difficult to enforce a punishment at the school level. Now outside authorities must be brought in for consultation. And their presence can sometimes lead to parental panic.

As educators of elementary, middle, and secondary school boys and girls, we realize that as young as kindergarten, children have crushes on other children. In some cases, changing hormones are an issue. When this happens, students may act in an inappropriate manner or do something that in the adult world would definitely constitute harassment. For example, a middle school child may stalk another student online, tracing the student's electronic movements in chat rooms, playing with his or her questionnaires, sending anonymous love e-mails, or otherwise invading the child's privacy. These actions are often the premise of every other 'tween television show, and the characters in sit-coms make it easy to do, but the school district may see the child's actions very differently.

Policy books written by teachers and administrators should include statements that prohibit the registering of another's student's name or setting up profiles without permission. The modern student may use information learned from electronic devices to get closer to a target student while in the learning environment. Therefore, your policies should review the school's stance on these issues. The policies should further address postings that can be viewed on school grounds, encouraging others to post nasty comments on another student's blog, and unauthorized use of another student's image, which is common after rejection. There should also be a policy for students who damage the reputation of faculty members with inappropriate blogs, e-mails, or Web pages that are for public consumption. Policies should be written to protect teachers with due process so that parents cannot send anonymous notes to administrators without their or their union's knowledge.

The next area that has to be addressed in a student handbook involves the First Amendment and its interpretation as it applies to schools. Under freedom of speech students have the right to voice their opinions. But what is your school or district's policy when a student posts bad reviews or feedback on or about another student without cause? New laws have recently been enacted trying to counteract these behaviors. They've forced schools to think of new policies and updates to be incorporated into their handbooks. For example, students who have posted images of naked students online or via cell phones have faced child pornography charges.

Your district should have a policy for Internet use. Does your handbook have a policy that would cover parents or students who repeatedly send e-mails to teachers harassing them to change grades or a report on the child? What if a student starts sending racist jokes using a school account and a teacher passes them on to a friend, who reports it to the school committee? What if the student takes it a step further and implicates a student's name in the jokes instead of the ethnicity—do you have a policy written to cover this action if the named student's family seeks legal remedy?

Harassment that involves physical assault also needs to be addressed. What does your policy book say about a group of girls deciding to play dodgeball? Probably there is nothing in your handbook, but now consider that these same girls decide to throw the ball only at one individual student, and the victim is pounded during a physical education class and is injured with bruises? How do you handle such a situation? In one case, a boy threw a water bottle at a girl's head when he found out she was bisexual and had practiced the Wiccan faith. The teacher documented it with student personnel, but little was done, leaving the student to feel unsafe in her school environment. This proved embarrassing for the school district when the affidavit, deposition, and other evidence that showed how a district protected the boy, a "blond, blue eyed superstar," from what should have been suspension, if not expulsion. Moreover, there will always be a record of his actions in the courts that can be dug up, but it would have been long forgotten had the school just dealt with him when he was a high school student.

There may even need to be a policy that covers financial forms of harassment. For example, if students begin bombarding a student's or teacher's cell phone with texts, spam, or messages for which the victim is charged twenty cents each by the phone service provider, this can be financially devastating to the victim! Also, bullies may take other children's lunch money, causing financial hardship to the family. A school must have a policy on reimbursement, protection, and alternatives to the extortion practices often found in today's school systems.

Here is a newer problem for the modern school administrator: During my tenure as a teacher, students often used cell phones to send threats to other students. Long gone are the days of passing notes. Electronic threats are the "in thing" to send and receive. The negative side to this is that teachers can be left unaware that harassment is happening in their classroom. Your handbook should incorporate a policy about sending threats to others during the school day, with varied consequences depending on whether the message is sent during a class, between classes, during a break period, or after school but on the school grounds.

Elementary schools should also write policies on bullying for students as young as kindergarten. For example, a kindergarten boy's mother complained to school authorities that a girl in his class had slapped him across the face and then pulled another girl's ponytail and told the boy that the same thing would happen to him if he told the teacher about her behavior. When I first heard the case, I was surprised, because who thinks about a violent kindergartener? The answer is today's administrator, who has to protect the district's interests! As we know, teachers generally handle situations within the classroom at that age, but in a litigious society, potential issues should be addressed in a handbook. And written policies shouldn't stop with addressing physical behaviors. Making fun of other students or teachers that leads to embarrassment, such as making fun of someone's physical traits, manner of speaking, or clothing, should also be addressed in the handbook, as it damages the victim in his or her learning environment. Policies should further include rules about the sharing of other students' contact information.

Also, policies should be written stating that if students overhear information about a student, they aren't allowed to repeat the information to other students. Kids innocently repeat things, but it can cause the child who is being talked about to be singled out, as in the case of a child whose parent is incarcerated.

As we have learned from the Columbine tragedy, creating or playing video games in which characters hurt, injure, or suggest the death of school personnel or people in the student body should be dealt with severely. This leads to the following section, which discusses the concepts of writing policies to address the possession or use of weapons on school grounds.

Weapons

According to the Children's Defense Fund and the National Center for Health Statistics, "In a single year, 3,012 children and teens were killed by gunfire" in the United States. According to the same government studies, this is "one child every three hours; eight children every day; and more than fifty children every week. And every year, at least four to five times as many kids and teens suffer from non-fatal firearm injuries."

Educational administrators must address weapon carrying or possession in schools. Federal law prohibits persons under twenty-one from buying handguns, but it does not prohibit kids as young as eighteen from possessing them. Weapons are not banned in every school across America, and state and local laws don't always prevent guardians from entering a school carrying a weapon! Reuters in 2008 reported that Texas was considering whether teachers could carry guns to school, and recently, the Harrold Independent School District unanimously approved it. This is the first district in America to allow teachers to have guns while teaching in schools. As school districts often pattern policies after one another, it is only a matter of time until the next district approves such a plan. Therefore, you must check your state's laws as you determine how your district wants to word its weapons policy. For example, the Brady Center has pointed out that the "state of Utah has argued for teachers and students to be given the constitutional right to bear arms." The prohibition of weapons on school grounds should be written into school policies and should be compliant with local, state, and federal laws. Fox News reported that in 2007 the state of Illinois "granted a firearms identification card to a ten month old baby." At this rate, preschools may have to implement policies for those tots who are "packing"!

Violent Acts

Schools are becoming more and more dangerous, and more students are becoming victims of violent acts in schools. Published statistical research states, "In 1933, 75 percent of deaths among youth between 15 and 19 stemmed from natural causes. Sixty years later, in 1993, 80 percent came from homicide and unintentional injury." (AMA, *Youth and Violence*, December 2000). Violence is a reality in today's schools. In 2000 the Josephson Institute reported that "88 percent of all boys and over 76 percent of girls surveyed said they hit someone in the past 12 months because they were angry." And a CBS report at the turn of the twenty-first century claimed that "22 percent of students knew of another student who carried a weapon to school." The same report alleged that "over 50 percent of the students polled believed that a school shooting could occur at their school." It is sad, but not surprising, that federal statistics indicate that "21 percent of middle school children reported fights or attacks in the United States in a single school year."

As educators it is our civic duty to protect the children in our care. It is essential that violent acts be recognized and reported by school districts in order for school security practices to improve. It is important to work with local law enforcement when writing these policies into your district's handbook. The school district's tolerance policies of individual acts should be clearly listed with penalties for violations. The handbook should also include a section that discusses your district's policy regarding violent acts committed against teachers. It should further include teachers' rights to press assault charges, expulsion consequences for such attacks, and a clause about potential criminal charges for violent acts.

Federal and State Regulations

This section provides the reader with basic definitions of state and federal acronyms and laws as published by the U.S. government (nces.ed

.gov/pubs97/p97527/Acronym.asp). As an educational administrator, you should be versed in these terms and have a basic understanding of how they apply to your district.

The **Individuals with Disabilities Education Act (IDEA)** ensures services to children with disabilities throughout the nation

The **Protection of Pupil Rights Amendment (PPRA)** seeks to ensure that schools and contractors make instructional materials available for inspection by parents if those materials will be used in connection with an ED-funded survey, analysis, or evaluation in which their children participate. This is the most important part to know: it also seeks to ensure that schools and contractors obtain written parental consent before minor students are required to participate in any ED-funded survey, analysis, or evaluation that reveals information concerning political affiliations; mental and psychological problems potentially embarrassing to the student and his or her family; sexual behavior and attitudes; illegal, antisocial, self-incriminating, and demeaning behavior; critical appraisals of other individuals with whom respondents have close family relationships; legally recognized privileged or analogous relationships, such as those of lawyers, physicians, and ministers; or income (other than that required by law to determine eligibility for participation in a program or for receiving financial assistance under such program).

Public Law 107-110 mandates that all children have a fair, equal, and significant opportunity to obtain a high-quality education and reach, at a minimum, proficiency on challenging state academic achievement standards and state academic assessments. This law is often used to help Native American children, poor school districts, and areas in need of assistance.

Public Law 108-446 was enacted to help handicapped children. It looks at remedies for equality.

Health Insurance Portability and Accountability Act of 1996 (HIPAA) protects the privacy of student health records.

The Equal Access Act (EQAA) applies only when the school has a "limited open forum," meaning the school recognizes "non-curriculum-related" student groups.

FAPE stands for "free appropriate public education," and it can be found under Section 504 of the Rehabilitation Act of 1973, as amended.

FERPA, the Family Educational Rights and Privacy Act, protects the privacy of student records. This law also examines due process. The U.S. Department of Education notes on its website the following information: "Schools may disclose, without consent, 'directory' information such as a student's name, address, telephone number, date and place of birth, honors and awards, and dates of attendance. However, schools must tell parents and eligible students about directory information and allow parents and eligible students a reasonable amount of time to request that the school not disclose directory information about them. Schools must notify parents and eligible students annually of their rights under FERPA."

Title Laws

Title I is the largest federal education funding program for schools. Its aim is to help students who are behind academically or at risk of falling behind. School funding is based on the number of low-income children, generally those eligible for the free and reduced price lunch program.

The aim of **Title IIA** is to increase student achievement through comprehensive district initiatives that focus on the preparation, training, recruitment, and retention of highly qualified educators.

Title IID is a federal grant program intended to help districts improve student achievement through the use of technology in their schools.

Title III is the section of No Child Left Behind that provides funding and addresses English language acquisition and standards and accountability requirements for limited English proficient (LEP) students.

Title IV, the Safe and Drug-Free Schools and Communities Act, supports programs to prevent violence in and around schools; prevent the illegal use of alcohol, tobacco, and other drugs by young people; and foster a safe and drug-free learning environment that supports academic achievement.

Title V promotes informed parental choices and innovative programs.

Title VI, part of the Civil Rights Act of 1964, outlaws discrimination based on race, color, and national origin for agencies or programs receiving federal funding.

Title VII usually deals with racial imbalance and involves compliance in the following areas, according to the Department of Education in Massachusetts: If it can be proved that there is work toward improving a racially imbalanced plan to improve the quality of education; if more than half of the pupils attending the school are defined as minority based on the Federal Emergency School Aid Act; if a district can show racial isolation; or if it is a magnet school facility and educational programs.

Title IX of the Educational Amendments of 1972 bans sex discrimination in schools receiving federal funds, whether it is in academics or athletics. For example, if the school buses the football team of boys to games but not the cheerleading team of girls, this can be a violation of Title IX. If a female student wants to play football or take part in wrestling or any other traditionally male sport, she can participate; likewise, a male student who wants to cheerlead cannot be denied. A male student who wants to join glee club or cheerleading cannot be denied based on gender.

Special Education Law

Administrators should be versed in special education law. According to the federal government's website, www.ed.gov, "In order to comply with the federal mandate [Public Law 102-119, known as the Individuals with Disabilities Education Act, Part B (34 CFR Parts 300 and 301 and Appendix C)] that all disabled children receive a free appropriate public education, a school district must provide special education and related services at no cost to the child or her/his parents." FAPE works in conjunction with the Americans with Disabilities Act (ADA), which is a civil rights law passed in 1990 that does not allow discrimination against people with disabilities in employment, public service, and public accommodations. Schools are required to comply with Individualized Education Programs (IEPs) and Section 504 plans under special education laws.

English as a Second Language (ESL)

The laws regarding English as a second language, bilingual education, and sheltered English immersion are very strict. For example, Title VI is violated by a school district if programs for students whose English is less than proficient are not designed to teach them English as soon as possible or if they operate as a dead-end track. Title VI has been interpreted by U.S. federal courts to prohibit denial of equal access to education because of a student's limited proficiency in English. Another law that you should be familiar with is the Equal Educational Opportunities Act (EEOA). This act was designed to require school districts to establish language programs and eliminate language barriers in schools. In 1981 the Fifth Circuit Court of Appeals, in *Castaneda vs. Pickard*, formulated a method to determine if a school district is in compliance with the Equal Educational Opportunities Act (1974). The three-part test includes the following criteria:

- "The school is pursuing a program informed by an educational theory recognized as sound by some experts in the field or, at least, deemed legitimate experimental strategy."

- "The program and practices actually used by [the] school system are reasonably calculated to implement effectively the educational theory adopted by the school."
- "The school's program succeeds, after a legitimate trial, in producing results indicating that the language barriers confronting students are actually being overcome."

Finally, district teachers and administrators must remember that under the law undocumented alien children cannot be denied a free public education, and school districts cannot inquire about the child's family's alien status.

Finding Educational Case Law

Case law is always changing, and almost all departments of education have a website page updating current laws or cases. The American Civil Liberties Union has an entire section of its website dedicated to school law and the protection of student rights. Most city and town libraries keep referenced volumes of state and federal laws. Currently, educational law websites are becoming more and more available on the Internet, helping you find the most recent cases.

The citation of a public law, such as Public Law 107-110, always begins with the words "Public Law." The numbers that follow these words indicate the session of Congress that enacted the law, followed by the sequential number of the law within this session. So, in this example, the law was passed by the 107th Congress, and it was the 110th law passed. Public Law 91-189 would be a law enacted by the 91st Congress and the 189th law passed.

Citations for court decisions follow a similar format. The citation for the case *Normdabro v. Southern Administration Dept. of Education*, 309 US 224 (1969), for example, indicates that the case was decided in 1969 and reported in volume 309 of the *U.S. State Reports* on page 224.

If the case was heard on appeal, you will find it in the *Federal Reporter*. If you read the citation for *Barlow v. Coombe County Board of*

Education, 91 F.2d 1313 (3rd Cir 1990), for example, you would know that the volume was 91, in the second series, on page 1313 for the U.S. Court of Appeals for the Third Circuit in the year 1990.

If it is a Supreme Court case, you might want to simply look it up at www.supremecourtus.gov.

You may also use research systems such as WESTLAW and LEXIS. Or for quick lookups, you can go to www.wrightslaw.com and review cases by subject.

Legal Wording for Field Trips and Other School-Sponsored Events

The school committees should determine the policy for all school sanctioned or sponsored events. A teacher may take a group of students to Scotland, but the trip may not be a school district sponsored event. The teacher then assumes any liability associated with the trip, unless the school in some indirect way made it possible for the students to travel on school time. Following are some considerations for your safety and well as for student safety:

- Make sure your district creates a policy for noncustodial parents' signatures. I have had cases where noncustodial parents have actually come to the classroom seeking to speak briefly with their child. Schools need policies of what to do in these situations that are clearly communicated to teachers, as well as to students and parents. Non custodial parents do not have the same rights as custodial parents. It is highly advised that guidance and the administration be made aware of any attempts by a parent to see a child before access is granted.
- If a school committee or administrator has not sanctioned the trip, teachers should not use school stationery or letterhead. An administrator may use letterhead to send parents a letter to the effect that the school has not sanctioned the event. The school has no obligation to contact or inform the

33

noncustodial parent. The noncustodial parent may not in some judgments be allowed access to the child and therefore may not attend school functions.

- State law may or may not require parental permission to leave school grounds, but most permission slips are not binding documents and can still leave a district and its chaperones open for possible litigation.
- The head chaperone should meet with parents and students ahead of time to set the ground rules for any trips.
- Never transport students in your private vehicle. If you release a student to ride with a noncustodial adult, make sure the person has been checked by Criminal Offender Record Information—widely referred to as "being CORI checked."
- If a school group is traveling, be sure all students' guardians have signed a medical waiver.
- Be sure to offer travel insurance, as school trips do get cancelled.
- Make sure that legal disclaimers for liability are predetermined.
- Make sure you have appropriate chaperones, as you are ultimately responsible for students' safety.
- School trips are considered a twenty-four-hour school day if away from your home school.

Chapter 2

School Documents

Documents are records that people keep as proof that something has happened. It is important as a teacher, or as an administrator that you document information on a regular basis. But many times, people aren't good at keeping records, and if they do, they aren't always accurate. Nothing is worse than scrambling to find paperwork or to prove something happened after the fact. If you plan to be effective in education, you must document and keep accurate records, so that if an issue arises, you can reference it back to the materials you saved. As an administrator, it is important that you emphasize to your faculty and staff the importance of keeping appropriate records. Here are some perfect phrases to use to help motivate teachers to do so:

Please make sure you are keeping accurate records.

I would like to ask faculty and staff to maintain copies of records.

In case of litigation, make sure you keep accurate records of dates, names, and times of meetings, as well as the substance of the communication.

Record keeping is important, and with that in mind I am going to ask you to . . .

When an incident occurs in your classroom, I would ask that you document it on this form.

Unfortunately, we are living in a society that litigates. To protect yourself and the district, we ask that you . . .

Recently, an incident arose, and we had no paper trail. I am going to need to insist that you . . .

Make sure that you maintain accurate records throughout the year.

Your records should be updated daily both on paper and in the computer.

Be aware that you may be asked at any time under contract to produce your grade book. Please make sure that you keep accurate and up-to-date records.

Documents should be locked in filing cabinets for security purposes.

Questions have arisen in regard to . . .

We will need to begin documenting incidents of . . .

Make sure on all official documents that you submit a copy to the office.

If you are involved in an altercation with a student, make sure to document the incident.

Write down your observations and tuck them away somewhere safe. You may be asked to comment on . . . , and having accurate notes would be helpful.

If you are going to document an incident, make sure to get the person's name, along with the date and time of the incident.

To protect yourself, as well as the district, please keep accurate documents.

Documenting is an important part of your daily job; please make sure you are keeping up with the paperwork.

Please do not share documents about students with other students or members of the community.

If in doubt, mail yourself a letter describing the incident, but don't open it. If unopened, it can be used in court as a record based on the stamped postmark.

Records can be requested by various parties. Please keep your records updated.

Please make sure you keep your comments objective and factual.

Perfect Phrases for ELL and SEI Populations

As you will learn in other chapters, documentation for English language learners (ELL) and sheltered English immersion (SEI) student records is reported to state and federal agencies; therefore it is important to be very careful how you state information. This section will offer you pertinent questions to ask parents of ELL and SEI students when trying to accumulate data for school documentation purposes.

The first rule of documenting information for ELL, bilingual, and SEI students is to know the terminology. Here are some basic terms and language fundamentals you may want to use in your documents as they apply to this population in a school district:

Achievement test. This type of test measures what students have learned from a given program. Achievement tests should be part of every language program, with specific attention paid to the language goals and objectives of the program. The tests must strive for flexibility in regard to the special needs of particular students.

Our district intends to use the achievement test to benchmark how much of the English language your child has mastered.

Your child's achievement test score indicates . . .

The achievement test score was designed to . . .

The student's achievement test score correlates with . . .

Communicative competence. The purpose of language is communication. We want students to achieve fluency and accuracy in a competent manner. Such competence can be broken down into four areas: grammatical, sociolinguistic, discourse, and strategic. *Grammatical competence* refers to the mechanics and structure of the language. Examples of this would be proficiency in vocabulary, sentence structure, and pronunciation. *Sociolinguistic competence* is defined as the language user's ability to speak and be understood in a variety of social environments. This is influenced by factors such as interpersonal communication, the purpose and expectation of such interaction. *Discourse competence* speaks to one's effectiveness with respect to combining grammatical forms and meanings as they relate to different types of writing and speaking. Finally, *strategic competence* is viewed as the ability to which one uses both verbal and nonverbal communication. This is particularly important as this often acts as a compensation for inefficiency in the above three competencies. It is important to note that English language learners may be competent in one area but not another.

The student is not showing the communicative competence hoped for by this time period.

We intend to keep you informed as the child's communicative competence increases.

The child is having difficulty being understood.

The child is having difficulty with interpersonal communication.

The child is having difficulty distinguishing between spoken and written English.

The child is showing _____ competence with his or her verbal and/or nonverbal communication.

The child is showing growth in the area of communicating with native speakers of English.

Communicative language teaching (CLT). This teaching method suggests an approach to second language learning that emphasizes the four competencies found in communicative competence.

Our administration promotes communicative language teaching as a methodology.

We emphasize the importance of four competencies to improve student language learning.

According to research, this method allows learners to . . .

The CLT approach to second language learning and acquisition has served to help students . . .

This approach offers learners an incentive to master English because it helps them in four competency areas.

The best way to increase student mastery of English is to use approaches like CLT.

Competence learning model. When we speak of specialized courses, we are referring to learning that takes places in essentially four stages. In the first stage, there is a level of unconscious competence, as the learners don't know how much of the language they are aware of due to outside influences. The second stage suggests conscious competence, as the learners think about what they can actually communicate functionally in the target language. During the third stage we proceed to a level of conscious competence in which the learners are able to perform in the language if they think about how to say something. Finally, after much practice language learners become unconsciously competent when they naturally begin to produce the language, much like native speakers.

We use the model to describe four essential stages in language learning and acquisition.

We want students to perform in the English language; this is why we use CLM as a model.

Delayed copying. This is a technique whereby the teacher presents a brief simple sentence to the students and allows time for the students to consider it before removing it from the board. The teacher then will ask the students to reframe the sentence.

We support faculty who promote student-based activities such as delayed copying.

The teacher has been using a delayed copying technique to help your child master the English language.

We find that delayed copying not only improves the child's language skills, but builds his or her memory skills as well.

The activity of delayed copying allows the language learner time to focus on the language.

Descriptive grammar. Prescriptive or descriptive grammar is similar to what we refer to as communicating in the vernacular.

The child has been taught using descriptive grammar.

We encourage language learners to communicate using the vernacular.

We prescribe teaching language through the use of descriptive grammar.

Interference. Interference comes about when one's primary language impacts the processing of the language being learned.

Your child's first language is interfering with the learning of the second language.

The teacher has noted that the student has first language interference issues that are affecting his or her English language learning.

The child is fossilizing elements from his or her native tongue. The interference is causing the child to have difficulty mastering or acquiring the second language.

The student is having language interference issues.

To improve language interference issues, we suggest . . .

Inter-language. This could be defined as a combination of two languages, as well as features uncommon to both languages.

The child is demonstrating the use of an inter-language to communicate.

The inter-language usage interferes with the student's ability to . . .

The inter-language usage has caused the student to speak in a pidginized form of the target language.

Interlocutor. This refers to the recipient of the speaker's message.

We have looked at the student's strategies with the interlocutor.

To improve understanding, we have worked to see if the message is being comprehended by the listener.

Intonation. This refers to the tonal fluctuation used, such as pitch.

The student is having difficulty with tonal fluctuation.

The student needs to work on areas of pitch.

We are increasing the number of intonation exercises that we are using in the classroom to better students' language abilities.

Due to the first language, the student is having difficulties with intonation.

Language content. Here we are speaking of the three components that make up language, which are structural or grammatical factors, phonological factors (sound features including intonation, word stress, rhythm, and register), and lexical or vocabulary factors.

Our curriculum focuses on language content.

Our language testing and curriculum centers around the structural and grammatical points of English.

Fluency in English. Fluency refers to speaking proficiency and consists of both production and comprehension. Production means the use of appropriate vocabulary, tone, grammar, and pronunciation. More specifically, this takes place in an interactive context.

The student is having difficulty with English fluency.

The student has mastered accuracy in the language, but is having difficulty with fluency.

We want your child to produce authentic language and to improve his or her fluency in English.

The student needs to use more appropriate vocabulary/tone/ grammar/pronunciation.

The more interactive contact with native speakers, the more likely your child's fluency will improve.

Although your child is fluent in spoken English, he or she is underperforming in other skill areas such as reading/writing/ speaking/listening.

Language learning requirements. This requires four areas of understanding. First, students must be exposed to the language, understand its meaning and structure, and must repeatedly practice it.

According to school district policy, our language learning requirements include, but are not limited to . . .

Our program's language learning requirements require learners to . . .

As English language learners need to be both fluent and accurate in a language, we strongly encourage the following language learning requirements: . . .

We require a prerequisite of language learning requirements before entering . . .

Metalanguage. Metalanguage refers to the tools whereby another language is described, considered, and analyzed.

Our faculty and staff have been examining the target population of students' metalanguage.

After looking at student metalanguage, we have concluded . . .

We have both analyzed and taken into consideration the metalanguage in order to describe . . .

Modeling. Using varying examples to communicate a point, this often takes the form of role-playing between and among the students in drill exercises.

We ask teachers to model proper English for nonnative speakers to repeat . . .

We use modeling as a guide to demonstrate proper forms of English discourse.

Modeling a language helps the learner to . . .

Especially in our sheltered English immersion programs, we encourage language modeling.

Native speakers. Native speakers speak the target language.

We try to pair English language learners with native speakers in the school.

We want to help your child achieve near native-like speech.

Needs assessment. An evaluation whereby the needs of the students are measured so as to best achieve the goals of the program.

We recommend that a certified ESL teacher perform a needs assessment test to see how the district can best serve the child.

In order to measure the student's language ability, we will be administering a needs assessment.

Nonnative speakers. People who speak a different language than the target language.

As the child is a nonnative speaker of English, the district recommends . . .

Nonnative speakers are more apt to . . . than native speakers.

Overcorrection. A maladaptive technique in which an overuse of correction impacts the students negatively.

Overcorrection can lead to student frustration.

Paradox of language acquisition. Some students have the ability to learn at a high level despite receiving a limited amount of feedback and instruction.

Your child has a natural ability to understand and learn languages.

Your child is what we refer to as a "paradox" in the area of language acquisition.

Passive vocabulary. Vocabulary students are aware of, but seldom use in speaking and writing.

The teachers have noted that your child has an extensive passive vocabulary but a very limited active vocabulary.

The teachers find the student's passive vocabulary allows for greater comprehension, but at the same time limits the student's progress in spoken and written forms of communication.

The student needs to turn passive vocabulary into active vocabulary.

Passive. The erroneous belief that learning language does not require active participation by the students.

According to teacher reports, your child is a passive learner.

Your child has to actively try to use the language.

Placement tests. Tests that are used to place students in particular programs.

We will be offering placement tests for students to enter our programs on _____.

We do not randomly select students for particular courses; all students are placed according to test scores.

Because your child does not speak English, we have had the placement test translated into your child's native language.

Prescriptive grammar. Grammar that is formal as opposed to grammar that is used on a daily basis. Prescriptive grammar consists of definitive structures and formats.

Your child is using informal English in class. We prefer a more prescriptive grammar.

As prescriptive grammar consists of definitive formats and structures, we suggest that your child begin to . . .

Proficiency level. How well a student can use a language. The most common descriptions are beginner, false beginner (has a background in grammar and vocabulary but is unable to communicate effectively in the language), advanced beginner, intermediate, and advanced.

The student's proficiency level is . . .

The student is not proficient in the skills areas of . . .

Based on what our experts have seen, we believe the student's proficiency level is . . .

The child shows a high proficiency level in the skill areas of speaking and listening but is not meeting the required proficiency levels in the areas of reading and writing.

Proficiency tests. A generalized test created to give an overall view of the student's basic level of proficiency in a subject area.

At the beginning of each academic year, we require students to take a proficiency test in the English language to determine what services are necessary.

We need to administer a language proficiency test to your child.

According to the proficiency test results, . . .

If you are documenting information or reading documents related to ELLs, bilinguals, or SEIs, you will probably need to be familiar with the following acronyms:

TESL: Teaching English as a second language (used in an English-speaking country)

TEFL: Teaching English as a foreign language (used in a non-English-speaking country)

TESOL: Teaching English as a second or other language

CAL: Center for Applied Linguistics (This organization has created and researched the SIOP Model that is used by many schools and districts across the United States.)

Limited English proficient (LEP): Students whose first language is not English and whose English language skills are not equal to those of their peer group

English as a second language (ESL): The teaching of English to speakers of other languages through a wide variety of methods

NAEP: National Assessment of Educational Progress

NCLB: No Child Left Behind

PEP: Personalized Education Plan

ESEA: Elementary and Secondary Education Act

ESL: English as a second language

FRL: Free and reduced priced lunch

GED: General education diploma

IDEA: Individuals with Disabilities Education Act
IEP: Individualized Education Program
AIP: Academic improvement plan

When discussing ELL, SEI, or bilingual students in curriculum-related documents, you may wish to speak about the methodology you are using in your district or classroom for reports. It is vital that age-appropriate methods or models of instruction are used. This section offers you the most appropriate choices for elementary, middle, and high school students.

TPR: Total Physical Response
Audio-Lingual method (also called the military approach)
SIOP model
Psycholinguistic approach
Grammar Translation method
Communicative method
Silent way
Direct approach
Functional-Notional approach

Perfect Phrases for Students of Differing Cultural Backgrounds

Compared to other populations in a school district, documenting the methodology and terms, as we have seen in the above instances, is far easier than documenting the actual student. As a school administrator you should be aware that federal law allows students who are without papers to attend public school. However, the nightmare for administrators is that they can't always get paperwork from students with illegal status because the family or child may fear being taken away or having their families deported. For documenting names and other basic types of information, we will look at a different approach, especially because the rules protect these children because the government knows they most likely will stay in the United States and not return to their original countries. As a longtime activist and promoter for immigrant care and language services, I offer some techniques you can use to help your district get the information it seeks. Here are some suggestions:

- Remember that there may be cultural differences between the American teachers and the immigrant student or the family. For example, in Western culture it is often customary to greet a person with a firm handshake and to look him or her in the eye, but this may not hold true for other populations. Referencing negative historical events or commenting on cultural or religious practices can often lead to major misunderstandings that cause divisions between learners, educators, and communities. The best advice is to err on the side of caution using professional and neutral language that doesn't pass judgment. For example, in some cultures greetings may come in the form of sticking out your tongue at the person, kissing, or bowing, most of which aren't common in Western public education settings.
- Remember parents may think your methods are like those found in their home country. They may associate positions with negativity because not all children are allowed to be educated in all countries. Parents may not understand why people of different skin colors, ethnicities, backgrounds, religions, and gender are allowed to study together or why certain topics may be taught.
- Remember family members may not be blood relatives, and sometimes all people in a community are known as the "auntie." Don't assume the auntie or uncle's address is that of a child's family by American terms. Also, it might be wise to do a mapping exercise, in which the child draws a map from the school to his or her home, because it may not match the address on the school's record.

- Remember kindness goes along way, as does a warm welcome. Immigrants have often faced adversity and may not trust Americans or other westerners, because many have been exploited by nationals on different levels.
- Remember immigrants may think educators require a bribe. Don't be insulted, but make sure that they understand that you want nothing from them, except to educate their child. In many countries, administrators and teachers are known to take money to make sure the child receives the lesson. In some languages, there are words for taking a payoff or for accepting a gift in order to influence a child's chances for being guaranteed a chance to learn or to pass a course. Assure the parents that this is not part of your school's curriculum and that all children are afforded a free and appropriate education.

There are other important concepts that as an administrator you will need to consider. For example, as our population becomes more diverse, so do our school districts.

This section seeks to address cultural sensitivities in greeting parents in more diverse school district populations. Making the initial connection is essential to building a good teacher/parent relationship. Here are some phrases that can help you meet the needs of parents:

Are you aware that the city/district/state offers you the following services free of charge or at a nominal fee?

What can you tell me about your son or daughter's education in his or her past school?

Did your son or daughter like the previous school?

Do you have any questions for us before we begin?

Do you need bilingual services?

Were language services offered in the previous school?

Do you need me to request a translator?

Do you qualify for any programs that we should be aware of?

Do you need help processing your paperwork?

Can we assist you in ways we might not be aware of?

Have you been given a copy of our manual for parents?

Is there anything we can do to help your transition?

Are you aware we offer sheltered English immersion programs?

Is this your first time in an American school system?

What can the school do to accommodate your needs?

What special accommodations are necessary for our meeting?

How do you think your son or daughter has adapted to American culture?

Likewise, other forms of cultural confusion might interfere with your understanding or the parents' understanding of the greeting. For example, in some cultures, the teacher is revered and the parents will not make eye contact with you. This is a cultural difference and should be understood and accepted as such. Miscommunication of gestures and greetings can lead to further difficulties. Thus, it is important that you know how and when to greet a student's parent on the night of the conference. For example, when greeting a fundamentalist Muslim male, I have learned that as a woman I do not shake his hand, but rather put my hand in a fist and move it up and down without touching him. When you become close with a family, you still learn when to keep your distance. For example, you don't hug a traditional Japanese person as a greeting.

As American culture doesn't always teach us how to work with people of other languages and cultures, I am sure you are wondering how you should approach these parents. Simply ask your ELL or SEI students before conferences what is and isn't appropriate. For example, find out if their parents were born in America or immigrated to the United States, or simply ask the students to fill out index cards with the following information so that you can plan your meeting accordingly. When preparing an index card for your Rolodex, it is important to ask the student to provide the following information:

Parent's legal name
Parent's preferred name
Custodial parent's name
Noncustodial parent's name
Contact information
Where were your parents or guardian born?
What is important to your parents?
Where did they go to school?
Are they working, and if so, where?
Are there any special things I should be aware of before meeting your parents?
What language are your parents most comfortable communicating in?
Does your parent require a translator?
What cultural differences should I know about?
Which language(s) can your parents speak?
Will a friend or family member attend with the parent, or should I request a translator?

Currently, it is estimated by the federal government that at least 11 percent of the children studying in America are enrolled in ESL or bilingual programs. However, if students are fluent in English or can participate in classes using the English language, they aren't usually listed in those types of statistics. This means the number of immigrant children studying in the United States is higher than those statistics indicate. These numbers suggest the likelihood of your district having students from one or more foreign countries as members of your school. Here are some simple recommendations to consider when thinking how to best communicate with nonnative speakers of the English language.

First, be aware of appropriate timing. Let's say you have a Japanese mother and an American father attend your meeting. It is unfair to address only one parent and treat the other as an invisible entity. Sometimes, because of language barriers, it is difficult to communicate with both parents, but it is important to make an attempt. Or be aware of cultural differences, such as how one perceives the hours of the morning. We know what the American concept of "morning" means for the father, but are you aware of what it means for the mother? The Japanese greeting for "good morning" should only be used before 10 A.M. It may sound odd to her if used at an 11A.M. appointment.

It is important to be yourself, yet be aware of your role. It is hard not to speak a pidgin form of the language because we think it is easier for the listener to understand. It is inappropriate to imitate a person who speaks with an accent. Although you might think it is helpful, it is not. Do not imitate an accent or use their slang, as this appears rude and presumptuous. This may well also engender a hostile response on the part of the parent.

It is important that you be seen as making an effort in your greeting. Misusing and/or mispronouncing words from a person's native language can make you appear inept. There are many online pronunciation dictionaries that can help you pronounce a word in a foreign language. If you pronounce these words wrong and someone points it out to you, it could be embarrassing, so try to learn the correct pronunciation! Imagine, the nonnative speakers in your classroom have to learn so many words in English, and all you are asked is to memorize one greeting in their mother tongue.

It is also important that teachers be aware of their gestures. If you are a person who gesticulates while speaking, it is best to consider how this behavior presents itself. I remember years ago, one teacher I worked with loved to give the thumbs-up sign. Well, he insulted students quite by accident because he was unaware that in many cultures this sign is a vulgar gesture!

Another common gesture that can often be misinterpreted is the American "okay" sign. Teachers often make the okay sign, using the index finger and thumb touching with the other three fingers upright. Like the thumbs-up sign, depending on the culture, it can have a negative, if not vulgar meaning.

If you are teaching Navajo students on a reservation, a firm handshake may be inappropriate. It is often suggested to make a less firm handshake. In contrast, Koreans and Japanese seldom shake hands, preferring to nod or bow. In Arab cultures, it is common to extend only the right hand when shaking hands. The simple rule to remember is that cultural sensitivity on your part is often reciprocated by those to whom it is directed.

It has been my experience that if you are greeting a Chinese parent, it is better to use flat open palms and not a pointed finger. It is considered highly offensive to put your fingers near your mouth or to use an overabundance of hand gestures, as this could be distracting.

As most districts are aware, it is estimated that one out of every ten people in America speaks Spanish as his or her primary language. Government reports estimate that almost half of the American population is Hispanic. Even though the parents and child may hold an American passport, they may demonstrate different cultural norms than those traditionally found in upper-middle-class white protestant suburbs. For example, the physical proximity of the initial greeting may be more intimate than you are used to. People of Hispanic heritage may also focus on interdependence more than independence. Sometimes when Hispanic parents greet a teacher of another heritage, the teacher may feel the parents are being inappropriate because they are entering the teacher's personal space. A suggestion that can be offered to those who wish to maintain more personal space is to set up the office or classroom so that a desk is between the teacher and the parents.

Districts usually provide translators by law, but teachers should make an effort to learn, at minimum, how to at least say hello during the greeting. This will put families more at ease. Remember, many parents without legal status may fear speaking to you due to their apprehension with respect to the Immigration and Naturalization Services (INS). You must assure the families that you will not release the information and affirm to them that under federal law the child is allowed to attend school.

Ask the translator ahead of time how to greet the parents in their native language in order to establish a relationship outside of the translator. You may want to ask the district translator to teach you how to say your name and teachers' names and subject areas as well. Sometimes just knowing a few simple words will get you all the cooperation and understanding that you need from the parents. This can make teaching their child much easier throughout the year when the support is present from the home. It is suggested that while the interpretor is speaking, the educator should continue to face the parent.

It might also be suggested that you dress appropriately for the parents' culture, and for women that may mean no short skirts or sleeveless tops. It may also mean no tucked-in shirts for women who are wearing formfitting pants, as it may cause offense. Your goal is to earn the family's respect, trust, and cooperation.

Perfect Phrases for Accreditation Documents

This is an area where your school cannot fool around or "wing it." When it comes to English language learners, make sure your records and paperwork have every *t* crossed and every *i* dotted. If you are documenting materials for an incoming accreditation team, the onsite team will require the school district's documentation regarding its English learner education programs and services. Although there is no set rule, and this information should always be ready at any time, it is recommended that your district make it available at least eight to twelve weeks before the visitors or evaluators come for an onsite visit. And don't be surprised if the evaluating staff requests follow-up information in order to clarify the submitted documentation. This is normal, and should not cause you panic. Remember that this is a paperwork-intensive area, where accountability is key, and most likely, this follow-up information is the missing piece that is necessary in order to rate a particular criterion. This is why you have to make time to get your documentation together for review. Most departments of education won't just show up and make a surprise visit unless a complaint is issued or there is an area of "concern." The evaluators, under normal circumstances, will give your district enough warning to prepare reports about ELL services available to the elementary, middle school, and high school students.

In the documentation, they will most likely ask you for the following:

- Limited English proficient (LEP) student roster including the grade level, school, and program model
- English proficiency level and native language of each LEP student
- A list of formerly limited English proficient (FLEP) students who have been transitioned to general education classrooms within the past academic year
- A separate list of the names of students who are designated LEP, but who as a result of an approved waiver are not in the district's SEI classroom or program
- A list of the students or parents who have agreed to "opt out" of an ELL program
- Copies of all screening and assessment instruments
- The names and qualifications of teachers used to evaluate and/or make placement decisions in English learner education programs
- Documentation of identification and evaluation procedures
- A separate list of all modifications that your district made
- A copy of the district's waiver guidelines and forms
- A description of programs implemented in response to waivers

- Copies of all approved and unapproved waiver requests (Where waivers have been granted, make sure you have the appropriate signatures based on the state requirements.)
- The names and qualifications of staff members responsible for the instruction of individual students based on language ability
- Copies of any means for documenting the parents' wish to "opt-out" of an ELL program and any forms used to monitor student progress
- A brief description of the district's ELL programs and services
- A copy of any written policies and procedures regarding the implementation of sheltered English immersion (SEI), two-way bilingual, or other English learner program for LEP students in the district
- The district's identification and placement criteria
- All procedures for exit criteria
- A description of the district's most recent program evaluation
- A list of improvements made based on evaluations to your language program
- A copy, in all required languages, of the sample notices sent to parents regarding: enrollment of their child in an ELL program
- A translated outlined description of the programs available
- Information regarding the ELL child's educational placement and progress
- A chart and a report of ELL student schedules including class credit values and the names of instructors
- A description of the monitoring process offered to former LEP students who have exited ELL programs (It is suggested this document include the names and qualifications of staff members responsible for the implementation of follow-up activities for accountability purposes.)
- Evidence that the district provides communication that parents of students understand

- Evidence that the district provides information about extracurricular activities and school events to LEP students in a language they understand
- A simple description of the means by which the district involves parents and guardians in matters regarding their children's education
- Documentation of outreach programs
- A list of parents of LEP students who have been involved within the district
- Notes on any interactions with mainstream teachers
- A list of languages spoken or understood by staff and faculty at the school

Make sure you read your state's guidelines, as some will require more and others less information than the list presented.

Perfect Phrases for Special Education Documents

Special education law was enacted by Congress and requires strict adherence to regulations that allow a free and appropriate public education.

- **Individuals with Disabilities Education Act (IDEA).**
  Administrators know that federal law has guided the delivery of special education services for students with disabilities since enactment of the Education for All Handicapped Children Act (Public Law 94-142) in 1975. This federal law dictates the availability of federal funding for states to provide a "free and appropriate public education" for every school-age child who is considered disabled. As veteran administrators know, it was later renamed the Individuals with Disabilities Education Act in 1990, and reauthorized in 1997, so that today

the act emphasizes even more services for children. For example, it now includes the quality of teaching and learning and the establishment of high expectations for disabled children. No longer can a district, administrator, or teacher ignore the needs of disabled children in their classrooms. They are required to adapt teaching to help the student succeed using modifications when appropriate. Following are some federal laws that all educators must be aware of, because the parent of a disabled child will learn of them through research and advocacy groups.

- **Free and Appropriate Public Education (FAPE).** This act requires that the federal government provide "free and appropriate public education" and is the premise of the federal Individual Disabilities Education Act (IDEA). FAPE must be provided at public expense, under public supervision, at no charge to the parents, and must be based on the child's unique needs and not on the child's disability. This is the area that always seems to get school administrators into trouble, because they don't want to follow it, citing budgetary restraints. For example, FAPE must align with a state's educational standards, and it further must be provided for children beginning at age three and continuing until the student has reached the age of twenty-two. Parents will argue that FAPE must also be provided pursuant to an individualized education program (IEP) or an individualized family service plan (IFSP), and although as an administrator you may not like it, they will be correct.

- **Individualized Education Program (IEP).** The Individualized Education Program is a written document describing a pupil's present educational level, specific services to be provided, behavioral interventions to be used, language and communication needs of the child, and the child's need for assistive technology. The IEP also sets goals to be attained and specifies how the goals will be evaluated. The IEP must focus on ensuring, to the greatest extent possible, student access to the general curriculum.

- **Individualized Family Service Plan (IFSP).** The Individualized Family Service Plan is written for young learners and doesn't always apply to even elementary school learners, as the document articulates the procedure necessary to support the transition of a child to preschool services, or other services that may be available, and these procedures only apply to the extent that they are appropriate.

- **Individualized Education Program team (IEP team).** According to the standards found in American education, the IEP team is charged with developing, reviewing, and revising the student's IEP. The team consists of the parent(s), the child (if appropriate), a regular education teacher, a special education teacher, an administrator qualified to supervise the provision of services, and/or an individual who can interpret the instructional implications of evaluation results. Other individuals who have knowledge or special expertise regarding the child may also participate as members of the team, as may another guardian. Parents are not obligated to agree with the findings of the district's IEP team. As an administrator, it is important to remember that parents can appeal the decision of the group or IEP team if they are dissatisfied with the school's findings or actions.

When documenting or commenting on special education issues, you may want to use the following phrases to make it clear that your district is in compliance:

The student is owed due process under _____ law.

The school is in compliance with state and federal laws as we have complied with FAPE by . . .

_____ is a follow-up from a functional behavioral assessment.

_____ is an evaluation. It can be specific to one problem area academically, or it can include . . .

_____ has been modified (adapted) to meet the needs and disabilities of special needs youngsters.

_____ is used to enable an individual with a disability to function better.

_____ will be used while screening out distracters to assess the student's ability to stay on task.

_____ is usually applied to the context of focusing.

A behavior intervention plan should also . . .

A certain amount of articulation difficulty is normal, so we would like to monitor . . .

Abstract processes represent higher-order cognitive/intellectual processes. Currently, your child is having difficulties in processing these concepts.

The adaptive learning environments program allows a student on an IEP to . . .

Adaptive learning environments will be made available to your child.

Advocacy and/or legal counsel is available.

An educational setting and program for students with learning and/or behavior disorders where the environment is adapted or altered to . . . is offered in the following contexts at our school.

The assessment or your child may include objective testing using standardized tests.

We look at the extent to which your child can voluntarily and actively . . .

You should be aware that in special education disputes regarding your child, a formal legal proceeding will take place and will be heard by _____, who will listen to both sides of the dispute and will render a decision based upon the state's regulations or statutes.

As the parent, you should be aware that the application of assistive devices and assistive services may enable the individual with disabilities to function better. Insurance in many cases will cover . . .

As the parent, you should know this information is confidential. The definition of "education records" has legal significance in terms of the privacy of your child's student records. If you have questions, refer to FERPA.

Our team intends to help your child "work around" interference from his or her disability to accomplish learning tasks by . . .

As you may or may not be aware, a public school district must attempt such a _____ plan, usually appended to a student's individualized education plan, before changing a student's placement to a more restrictive environment, unless, of course, there is a . . .

Assistive devices can be used to help your child.

Assistive technology is available for your child.

At your child's chronological (actual) age, children are generally able to . . . , but your child currently can only . . .

Attention issues have been noted by the child's parents.

Before you grow concerned, may I preface the following statements by saying that sometimes performance deviates from the average. Sometimes additional services are necessary to meet the individual's needs when exceptional students are identified.

Your child's behavior intervention plan (BIP) consists of . . .

Can we discuss the developmental disability?

Can we talk about the developmental delays we have noticed in your child?

Certified occupational therapy can be made available for your child. This therapy will . . .

Criterion-referenced assessment will be used. Understand that this is a method of assessment in which the individual's score is compared to an established cutoff score.

Due process procedural safeguards are put in place to protect the child's (and the parents') rights in terms of . . .

Each state must have a policy as to how it will accomplish . . .

I understand your concern, but while all states are mandated to provide special education services to students who perform at substantially lower than the average level, not all states mandate services to those who are . . .

If the child does not "outgrow" certain problems, evaluation by . . . is indicated.

If you have concerns, you can contact the admission, review, and dismissal (ARD) committee. This is the education agency committee that determines whether a student is in need of special education services, and if so, what services.

If you wish to appeal our decision, you may contact the state's department of education.

If your child has problems with central auditory processing, we can . . .

In general, behavior that enables the individual to "fit in" with his or her environment and peers results in . . . . As it applies to your child, we want to note . . .

In order to comply, we will be using assistive technology to . . .

In order to identify children in need of special education services . . .

In your child's IEP we have noted an inability to perform coordinated movements.

May I take a moment to explain to you the different requirements that local education agencies have in terms of the range of settings available to educate students, including the mainstream classroom, regular (mainstream) with push-in services, mainstream with pull-out services, self-contained special classes, and homebound instruction.

May we recommend the following special needs advocate?

Modifications for the child will include . . .

Our district follows/refuses to follow one approach, which is to group students in special classes on the basis of the severity of their needs rather than on their diagnoses or educational classification.

Our long-range goals will include . . .

Our strategies emphasize remediation/accommodation of . . .

Public Law 94-142 is a part of federal legislation passed in 1975. It makes public education free for all handicapped children in the United States.

Sometimes central auditory processing disorder will result in a student...

The department of social services offers programs that provide financial assistance for needy children whose parents have abandoned them or who are unable to support them.

The descriptor can be applied to materials in order for us to adapt the curriculum to...

The EHA allows your child...

Under the Americans with Disabilities Act (1990), we are required to...

We are in compliance with...

We are not yet in compliance because...

We can offer you a case management service. This is a service usually seen only in cases where there are many needs or different services or providers requiring coordination and oversight.

We have measured in years, months, and days, as opposed to "mental age."

We have noted social or behavioral functioning.

We plan to formalize _____ so that it targets specific behaviors for alteration.

We prefer the word challenged *instead of _____.*

We will automatically accommodate...

We will be using observational methods and/or interviews.

We will include what environmental or proactive changes the staff will make.

We would like to put your child on a Section 504 plan. That means your child will receive an individualized plan that will specify what accommodations and/or services he or she will get from the school in comparison to nondisabled peers.

We would like to put your child on an Individualized Education Plan or IEP. Under federal and state laws the following accommodations can be made for your child: . . .

We would like to test your child for attention-deficit/ hyperactivity disorder.

When your child's entire educational program, including all related services, is provided in a separate location or special education school, it means that your child is entitled to services that may or may not include . . .

Would you mind keeping a log of your activities?

Your child has difficulty with nontangibles such as concepts, ideas, images, and symbols.

Perfect Phrases to Describe Differences in Learning

Children are different. Some students are visual learners, auditory learners, or kinesthetic learners. To avoid lawsuits you want to keep your comments factual and objective. Information can be misinterpreted, so you want to keep your written comments limited to general statements, and go further in depth with oral communication. Here are some phrases to help you describe differences within a professional context:

The learner does not demonstrate an ability to understand relationships and to recognize . . .

The learner does not meet eligibility requirements under state law.

The learner does/doesn't match the abilities of students in the traditional environment.

The learner has been recommend for . . .

The learner has difficulty with abstract reasoning.

The learner has difficulty with concrete/abstract items.

The learner has dyslexia.

The learner has dyspraxia.

The learner has emotional and behavioral disorders.

The learner has limited response or adjustment to . . .

The learner has trouble with fine motor skills.

The learner has trouble with gross motor skills.

Another way of saying that the learner is acting immaturely is to say that he or she is not behaving in age-appropriate ways; this is why we are suggesting . . .

The learner is eligible for adaptive physical education in order to help him or her . . .

We understand that this is a limitation related to a disability.

The learner is having problems with age-appropriate . . .

The learner is developmentally disabled in the area of . . .

The learner is suspected of having a behavior disorder.

The learner may be eligible for what is known as an extended school year.

The learner may be removed from the program if . . . is shown.

The learner may have a disability.

The learner may need to meet with . . .

The learner may need an evaluation of aural (hearing) processes.

The learner meets the needs/limitations of the . . .

The learner shows significant hearing loss.

The learner shows signs of being emotionally disturbed.

The learner's active range of motion includes . . .

The learner's neurological dysfunctions are causing him or her to . . .

The learner's sensory input or stimulation is . . .

The level of actual accomplishment or proficiency your child has achieved is . . .

The methods of . . . are suggested, but we need your permission to . . .

The movements required for handwriting are proving difficult for your child. Therefore, we would like your child tested or served . . .

The plan is supposed to be based on positive inducements, if possible.

The process of focusing has proven difficult for the learner.

The school is suggesting a behavior intervention plan.

The student has problems using expressive language.

The student may be eligible for speech and language services.

Perfect Phrases for Documentation of Classroom Activities

Administrators need to oversee that their classroom teachers are keeping proper records. Following is a list of some of the types of things you should be certain that your teachers document on a regular basis. By making sure your teachers cover this list, you will be prepared if anything should happen in a courtroom situation.

Seating
Roll call (including taking mark books outside during fire drills)
Absence records
Calling or recognizing pupils
Setting goals
Socialization
Tardiness
Excuses
Communication during school
Entering and leaving habits
Collecting and giving out of papers
Cleanliness of staff, students, educators and the building
Conditions of books and materials owned by the school district
Meetings with students
Lesson plans
E-mails and other correspondences
Passing to classes
Following bells and signals (Does the teacher let students out of class early?)
Following structured routines (Does the teacher let students come and go?)
Conduct
Leaving the room
Professional relationships
Quizzes and examinations (Records marks throughout the quarter and not a day before grades are due.)

Further, it is important to document the types of activities teachers use, so that students can't say, "we never do anything in that class" after receiving a poor grade. Here are general activities that classroom teachers use to help teach students how to master materials, so that your faculty members can check off those which they have used in case you have to show that your faculty is actively teaching student-centered lessons:

Application forms
Arts and crafts
Big books with big print
Blank books
Books with pictures, such as illustrated dictionaries
Books on CD
Brochures
Bumper stickers
Business cards and materials
Business debates that can be uploaded to URLs
Calendars
Cartoons
Charts, graphs, and other plotted information
Comics
Computer lab
Computer software and programs
Cookbooks
Costumes and props
Daily planners
Desktop publishing
Displays
Easels
E-mail
Electronic media
Freeware programs (such as Audacity, a freeware system for
    digital voice recording)

Felt story boards
Fund-raising drives
Games and activities
Greeting cards
Highlighted materials
Illustrations
Information resource books
Instructions and directions (illustrated)
Internet access
Journals
Laser pointers [outlawed in some districts for
    safety purposes]
Letters
Pen pal scenarios
Library resources
Magazines
Magnetic letters
Manipulative letters
Manipulative objects
Maps
Media
Message boards
Murals
Newspapers
Notes
Nursery rhymes
Pamphlets
Pattern books
Pictures
Play scripts
Pocket charts
Poetry, rap, and chants
Posters
Product labels

Puppets
Recipe cards
Reference books
Schedules
Science fair
Sentence strips
Signs
Songs
Stick-up papers
Student-generated quizzes
Student presentations
Take-home activities
Telephone books
Textbooks
Twitter or texting services
Venn diagrams
Voice-recognition software
Web page development
Word cards
Word frames
Word puzzles
Word strips

Perfect Phrases for School Committee Reports

As an educational administrator, you will need to report to the school committee or board of education in your district. If you have to explain funding issues to teachers, you may want to use a phrase such as the following:

The school committee determines overall school department policy and budget.

But if you are discussing the school committee in general or reporting back on a recent meeting with the board, the following phrases can prove useful because they don't say whether or not you agreed with the decisions. They are factual points that will satisfy the public on a variety of levels without putting you as the administrator in an awkward position.

> *There will be a meeting of the school committee and the subcommittee on . . .*
>
> *The board voted to close public comment.*
>
> *The superintendent raised a question on whether students will be . . .*
>
> *The board voted to begin accepting applications in district from internal and external candidates.*
>
> *The school committee authorized the school department to develop a draft request for proposal (RFP) to retain a search firm in connection with . . .*
>
> *The committee voted to convene in executive session to discuss strategy for collective bargaining.*

Perfect Phrases for Describing a Safety Situation

All schools should have a policy outlining safety procedures to be followed, especially in the situations listed below. A school district should have policies that cover all foreseeable emergency situations. Policies may need to be reviewed and updated on an annual basis. Some states require that a school district submit a published handbook that includes policies and regulations to the state for review and approval. This section lists phrases to discuss common emergencies that occur in school districts. Here are some phrases to use when documenting an event:

Staff was called to a Code Red.

Staff contained students in a lockdown.

Student participated in an evacuation.

Students were taken off school grounds.

Student behavior led to an actual emergency.

Students were made to stay in a secured area.

Students blocked an evacuation exit.

Student encountered a blocked exit.

Doors and windows were/were not closed before the fire drill.

Teacher did not bring roster outside of building during emergency.

Students went into a lockdown mode.

Student refused to leave the classroom after an incident that endangered a staff member or students.

The school was not in compliance with fire laws.

A smoke bomb exploded. As a result, the fire alarm was set off in the main office.

The following public services were contacted in a timely manner: . . .

A fire was set in the building.

When the drive-by shooting occurred . . .

Only one main entrance to the school is in use during the school day, and visitors must press the buzzer to be admitted.

All visitors must sign in at the office.

Two-way communication devices between staff and the building are in use when outside on school grounds.

Lockers were searched because . . .

Vandalism occurred . . .

Perfect Phrases for Crisis Management Reports

Crisis management has become a serious and ongoing issue that has faced administrators and teachers over the years. If you are working in a school, it is not uncommon that a child commits suicide, a teenager dies in a drunk-driving accident, a shooting or stabbing occurs, a child is sexually assaulted, or a family member of a student is hurt or dies. When these things occur you have to be the strong face of the situation and use words that deescalate hysteria and breakdowns, because in schools patterns start to emerge because children have difficulty coping with grief. Here are some phrases to aid you:

We are making grief counselors and psychologists available to students at this time.

We are unsure of . . . at this time, but school officials will be negotiating in the best interests of the welfare of the children involved.

Our district has put together a crisis management team who will serve to . . .

We will offer free crisis counseling teams to students.

With the number of parental kidnappings that occur each year in this country, it is important that no child be released to the wrong person. This is why we have put together the _____ plan as a proactive measure.

We request that people remain calm and focused.

Try to lean on your friends and school community during this time.

If you feel isolated, we have counselors that you can talk with . . .

There will be an investigation into the scandal.

It is with heavy heart that I inform you of the passing of _____.

We offer our deepest condolences to the families and will offer continued support to them during their time of need.

We have no comment at this time, as we are still in the process of gathering information about . . .

Perfect Phrases for School Handbooks, Policies, and Procedural Guides

For legal purposes school handbooks should contain the policies and procedural guidelines for a school and its district. These handbooks should cover all types of policies and have legal clauses for issues that will occur, but may not yet have become an issue. For example, ten years ago, school handbooks never needed to make statements about sending out images of naked classmates, which now with the use of cell phone cameras has occurred and may even lead to charges of child pornography. A sample handbook statement for legal purposes might read as follows:

This publication summarizes many laws, policies, regulations, and practices that are important to Washington Harvard Public Schools (WHPS) students and their parents and guardians. It is not intended to be a complete directory of all laws and policies relating to students and parents. Federal and state laws and WHPS policies, regulations, and practices at the system-wide and school building levels are subject to change.

These phrases are written to help you direct students, parents, and people from the community to your book of guidelines:

Please refer to the parent and student policy handbook that was distributed to you on/at _____ .

To families and students: This publication contains important information. Please read it and sign both sides of the parent and student agreement in this packet and return it to the school.

Please refer to the parent/student agreement and the sections on equal education opportunities, procedures for enrollment, ELL support, student attendance, safety and health, transportation, the code of student conduct, student discipline and due rights procedures, search and seizure, privacy rights, promotions, and graduation policies found in the student handbook.

Our policy handbook contains important information on the promotion policy, school attendance, the code of student conduct and student discipline, the policy on acceptable use of the Internet, nondiscrimination policies, student records, student transportation, the care and return of textbooks and library books, and other school rules and policies.

Chapter 3

Conducting Efficient Meetings

Educational administrative meetings can either be productive or painful. If you want to conduct an efficient meeting, you may want to set ground rules. You have to take charge of the faculty just as they must manage their students in the classroom. There is nothing worse than sitting through a meeting in which colleagues or administrators beat a dead horse. As the facilitator of the meeting, you must be able to rein in conversations about subjects that cannot be solved, don't affect the whole group, or that are simply off-track from the agenda. Here are some phrases that might be handy to help control large groups of faculty during your meetings:

Before we begin I would like to set some ground rules.

We will be strictly adhering to the agenda today.

Thank you for being prompt to the meeting. May we begin?

Take a moment and read over today's agenda.

The meeting is set for _____ minutes.

Do we have any items that need to be added to the agenda?

I trust you will support each other and show respect when someone is speaking.

In order to identify new needs for our committee, we will be making a list of future action items to discuss at our upcoming meetings.

Today's meeting will follow this path: . . .

It only makes sense that today's meeting focuses on . . . and not . . .

I will need to steer side conversations and unsanctioned items away from today's meeting.

I will keep alert to any conflicts that may arise during the meeting, but I will not have them debated in the interests of time. We can discuss these conflicts at a later scheduled date.

As time is precious, this meeting will end at _____ P.M. Please be respectful of the time if offering a comment.

This meeting will monitor _____ accurately against objectives such as . . .

If we could channel our attention to the items at hand . . .

Today we will enforce a strict time limit on questions and answers in order to address the issues listed on our agenda.

Perfect Phrases for Taking Minutes

The point of taking minutes, or detailed notes, is to record a meeting in the most general manner without pointing to anyone in particular or reflecting negatively on any individual participant. Minutes from meetings should be transparent, but usually they are on a restricted distribution list. Minutes are only referred to when someone wants to get at something or someone. Otherwise they are tucked away in a binder never to be looked at that closely.

Although common sense tells you this defeats the purpose of minutes, it is the reality of minutes in most academic institution. They are a motion that people just follow through with to cover themselves in an audit or to document phases of progress.

Minutes must be accurate. When you are assigned to take, write up, and distribute the minutes, there are some things that you should do:

- Take attendance.
- For those invited but not in attendance, instead of writing, "They didn't show," be more diplomatic: "Apologies from [list the names]."
- List the date, room, and time period of the meeting and the name of the person conducting the meeting.
- List the agenda items.
- If necessary, add the category "items added to the agenda" for topics that did not make the publications but all agree to discuss.
- List "new items for business" in a separate section of the minutes to distinguish topics from past meetings.
- Bullet-point the topics.

Here are some phrases to use:

It was suggested that Mr. Phil Quirke would lead the next jamboree event for the district.

Dr. Leah Bornstein hopes to begin recruitment soon.

Dr. Steve Allison requested teachers to volunteer for . . .

Teachers will be asked to . . .

If an item is important, you should highlight or boldface it and refer to it as an "action item." This lets people know that it is of importance and needs to be dealt with quickly.

There are words and phrases to always avoid: for example, "The _____ was awful." Make every effort to make negatives into something neutral. Don't use names with negative comments: "Jayden Flynn suggested it was the direct fault of the special education department." Don't use someone's name with an accusation. Don't use the word *everyone*: "Everyone hated the idea." Instead, say it was "unanimous" and change the word "hate" to "strongly disagreed with" or "disliked." Don't quote people: "Mr. Broder said, 'The whole school event was just one big mistake.'" You have just made Mr. Broder enemies by using his name with that type of statement. His comments could haunt him and will prevent people from speaking up in the future. It is better to rephrase it to say something like this:

"It was felt that the event should be rethought before future implementation."

The rule of thumb is "never say *never*": "Ms. Cook mentioned that she never intended to help out with an event like that again." It is better to rephrase it to say something like this:

Next year, new committee members should serve on the committee, as past members will be retiring.

The sentence "Nothing was accomplished on the issue of _____" suggests that the committee couldn't function. You can phrase this in a better way:

The committee did not come to a resolution on the topic of _____.

The sentence "The committee worried in case someone might get hurt and sue us" is offering suggestions that could give people ideas that are not in the school's best interests. It would be far better to phrase it like this:

The committee discussed liability issues in regard to the event. The chairperson will confirm details with the school's business manager/insurer/legal department.

The word *problem* is a problem because of its negative nature: "The committee discussed all the problems." Such issues should be called *challenges* because this suggests that they will be overcome.

Sometimes, depending on the situation, you may want to refer to the minutes before the final distribution as something like the following:

A draft of the minutes

A summary of the unedited minutes

A log of the minutes before finalization

Closed distribution list of the draft of the minutes

When writing minutes for a faculty meeting, department meeting, supervisor meeting, and/or parent meeting, have the minutes vetted by someone neutral who was there. Remove any finger-pointing, negativity, or inappropriate wording. If you choose to use a name, do so with a positive statement, such as the following:

Mike Galliher's achievement was credited for . . .

Rosie McLaughlin and Elaine Plumb were actively involved in . . .

Peter Gregory and Norm Breault developed a program to attain . . .

Suzanne Harrison and Leullen Fox showed evidence of achievement . . .

Experience and expertise was offered by Dawn Hertzberg.

A positive impact was felt by . . .

John Canning offered the district a positive . . .

Members of the committee [list names] second the impressive involvement of . . .

Planning committees will consist of . . . [list names]

Transferable skills were noted and the following people volunteered their expertise: . . .

Perfect Phrases for Faculty Meetings

Faculty meetings are a necessary contractual item for the betterment of the educational process, but if not led properly they can be a disastrous meeting of the minds in which nothing gets accomplished and complaints flourish. I would like to begin this section with simple advice to administrators: faculty meetings can turn into town hall meetings, if not controlled. As educators, we have watched a simple meeting turn downright nasty at least once in our careers, because the meetings are usually scheduled at the end of the week at the end of the day, when people are tired and just want to get home. This, coupled with the fact that most union representatives want to speak after the meeting because all teachers and/or administrators are gathered, can cause sides of people's personalities to surface that might not otherwise appear.

When running a faculty meeting, it is essential to take attendance twice, at the beginning of the meeting and again at the end, because teachers sign in and leave. When running a faculty meeting you often have to address issues with teachers, just as you do with students, because in meetings they will grade papers, doodle, read a book, or hold side conversations. You must make sure that teachers take faculty meetings seriously. It is your time as the administrator when you can talk with your staff as a whole. Avoid always choosing the same leaders, and avoid making teachers work on projects for the school that are never used. Otherwise, they will tune you out, tell you what you want to hear, and go about their business with no change or progress taking place.

Running a faculty meeting is an art. You need the meeting to be short, sweet, and to the point. Hand out any information that can be read instead of spoken. Speak on only the things that you can't put in writing or don't want traced back in years to come. If you are conducting a faculty meeting, here are some suggestions:

- Send reminders to teachers well in advance and make the meeting date set, such as the third Thursday of the month. This helps to avoid scheduling conflicts and allows your meeting to take priority. Make sure that meetings are scheduled on school grounds and not in restaurants that serve alcohol, as tax payers may frown upon such scenarios during contracted time.
- Distribute important information in writing.
- Stay on topic and walk around the room to help keep the teachers focused on the meeting.
- Use good judgment in selecting proper modes of communication.
- Use visual aids and involve the faculty with issues that are relevant.
- Compliment people and departments with what they have done right, and speak privately to them about what they have done wrong.
- Make each member of the faculty think you are speaking to him or her directly.

If you are addressing faculty, you may want to use the following phrases during your meeting:

I am not sure if you are all aware, but I would like to give you a quick FYI about . . .

A quick note that you might find of interest: . . .

Money might be available for . . . [then watch all the heads perk up in shock].

Give me a minute to give you this information that you are going to need.

Take a moment and jot down these reminders.

Today we must cover _____. If we can do so without side conversations, I think we will end earlier than expected.

Perfect Phrases for Community Meetings

Community meetings are very important, especially because the community pays the tax dollars that fund your school and its programs. You want to put on your best image to the community and make people feel as if the school you run is a very positive place, despite the problems or challenges it may face. Here are some phrases that welcome community members to your school:

I want to express my pleasure for your being with us today.

I want to recognize those of you who came this evening to support . . .

I am so glad you chose to accept our invitation to join us this evening.

We are blessed with our community members in the _____ today.

Thank you for the generous time, money, and effort you as a community have offered our school.

It is a pleasure to welcome you to our school.

I am thankful to be able to work in a district with such a supportive community.

You are a great source of strength and support for our children and our school district.

Your goodwill and endless contributions to our school have made quite the difference.

I know I should convey a sense of modesty—but I am so proud that you came out to support us.

The sustained efforts from this community have helped us to . . .

You are a firm foundation of role models for the students who attend our community schools.

Perfect Phrases for Program Meetings

If you are meeting about a program, it is important that you learn how to phrase the standards that have built the program. Here are some phrases to use when conducting program-based meetings:

Can we take a moment to focus on our mission statement?

I would like for us to take a moment and examine the standards used in our _____ program(s).

We need to think about our program structure, its administration, and future planning to sustain it.

Let's assess the curriculum and instructional materials used with the _____ program.

I would like to discuss the instruction used with the _____ program in today's meeting.

Learner recruitment, intake, and orientation are the focus of today's meeting about our program.

I would like us to look at how we assess and evaluate our current programs.

Take a moment to read our program narratives.

I would like to suggest a program self-review using this instrument.

Can we overview the standards, aims, and objectives of our _____ program?

Today's meeting will describe the issues to be considered for developing new program standards.

Let's break down the current components of our program to see what issues need to be addressed.

Let's look at what practices have been effective in our programs.

Can we outline any case studies that might reflect our program's outcomes at today's meeting?

Perfect Phrases for Unplanned Meetings

Only schools depicted in the media have perfectly scheduled meetings; for schools in the real world unplanned meetings seem to be a way of life, since some parents and students drop in on teachers and administrators without warning. An incident may occur that requires you to call an unplanned meeting, and when it does there are phrases you can use to get through these moments. Here are some helpful examples:

A meeting wasn't scheduled for today, but we could make time right now to discuss the issue of concern.

I wasn't planning on meeting today about this issue, but since you are here, . . .

Thank you for dropping by. You are lucky I happen to have a few minutes to discuss this with you.

Please sit down, and I will be with you in a couple of moments.

Since we didn't plan to meet today, I can only give you a few minutes. Is it possible to give me a quick summary of your concerns?

I have a few seconds if you want to meet briefly before my next appointment.

We don't have an official meeting scheduled, but we could use this time for an unofficial fact-finding moment.

I would love to meet with you right now, but I already have another appointment waiting. Can you send me an e-mail, and I will be sure to schedule an appointment with you?

With my busy schedule, I don't have time for drop-in meetings. Could we meet next _____ instead?

Perfect Phrases for Meetings with Student Groups

Student groups need guidance. When addressing student groups, it is important that you keep some legal concepts in mind in order to protect yourself and the district from a lawsuit or parental complaint to the school board. Here are some legal concepts to keep in mind:

- A CORI-checked adult (checked for criminal record) must supervise any student groups that meet at the school.
- Courts have ruled that a school can deny student groups access when the school prohibits all student clubs or when the club is noncurricular and the school only permits curriculum-related groups.

- The equal access act applies only to secondary schools and not elementary schools.
- Secret societies and undemocratic organizations can be prohibited from meeting in public schools.
- Groups that fail to comply with reasonable regulations can be prohibited.

Knowing the laws can help you to phrase your wording carefully to students who may approach you seeking to have a group that meets at your school. Here are some perfect phrases that you can use to address the leaders of student groups:

Our school follows the Equal Access Act of 1984.

The EAA does not limit the authority of administrators to prohibit extracurricular organizations.

I am happy to speak with you about the issues involving schools and their powers to limit freedom of association.

Courts have ruled that the First Amendment does not allow educators to act as thought police.

Chapter 4

Evaluations

Educational systems rely on evaluations to improve programs as an objective determination of the merit, worth, and significance of something or someone using criteria against a set of standards. However, as educators know, evaluations are often subjective and may not accurately reflect the truth. Further, since evaluations are used to characterize and appraise subjects of interest in a wide range of areas in an educational environment, it is not surprising that faculty, parents, and the community often question them. As an educator, it is essential that you organize the categories of your evaluations with facts and not broad statements, so that if one is suspected of not being a fair appraiser of a program or person, it doesn't taint the other standards of measurement used. Here are some simple and basic areas for evaluating faculty that are used in schools for evaluative purposes.

Personnel of the student body
Physical needs of the school
Social needs of the school
Vocational needs of the school
Setting teacher goals
Measuring teacher performance

Measuring staff performance
Measuring school effectiveness in various areas
Determining and providing intellectual endowment
Determining and providing for academic achievement
Understanding curriculum and assessment
Supervision of classroom teachers
Special types of school work
Understanding the daily program
Reporting of incidents required under one's license
Professional behavior in and out of the classroom (as defined by
    the collective bargaining contract or agreement)
Training the student body
Dealing with nonconforming pupils
Problems with management
External relationships
Renewal of contracts
Committee work
Student evaluations of teacher performance
Supervisory work

As noted above, evaluations in school districts take on many forms. It is important that you keep your comments factual on observations. For example, a teacher who grieves an evaluation because the principal has written, "People complain that she is not a team player" could argue to have such a statement removed, clarified, or questioned for multiple reasons. Let's look at some:

- What people? There are no names and no written complaints that have come to the teacher's attention before the instructor received the evaluation. Citing anonymous people or the suggestion thereof is just begging for a potential lawsuit.
- Is *complain* the correct word? Consider if the person who allegedly said this would use the word *complain* if sworn to an affidavit or deposed. Maybe he or she would retract and claim

the words were said in passing, general comment, or on an off day.

- What does it really mean to be a team player? This was a bone of contention during a whistle-blower lawsuit, when the teacher argued that she couldn't play on the "team" of the administration because their actions were endangering the health, welfare, and safety of children. Moreover, the teacher claimed that the evaluator meant the team of teachers that the principal favored, who were willing to act in an unethical manner, which the educator felt could be a violation of her license.

Instead, evaluations should be written using tangible and objective statements. Below is an example of how the statement might have been reworded:

On March 3, 2008, the chairperson of extracurricular activities, Ms. May Wood, reported that the teacher had missed four practices (on February 19 and 28 and March 1 and 2), despite being paid by the district as the advisor. The teacher was given a verbal warning, as well as her due process rights, on March 4, 2008, by Principal Wilson and Assistant Superintendent Alexander. After she again missed practice on March 18, 2008, a written reprimand was sent to the teacher (see attachment 1). Instead of working with the administration, the teacher cornered Ms. Wood during a parent conference and began verbally accosting her for informing the administration of her actions (see attachment 2). As a result, we have filed a report for the teacher's dismissal from her position as a school advisor (see attachment 3). It has come to our attention that the teacher has refused to take part in further school activities. Therefore, we feel she has not performed as a team player.

As an administrator, it is also important to remember that courts have ruled that supervisors generally have what is called "qualified privilege" to comment on matters concerning the operation of the school, provided they are working in good faith. This privilege can also extend to letters of recommendation. For example, if Mr. Doe is fired for child molestation charges and he applies to another district, the superintendent would not be held liable for stating a fact, such as "Mr. Doe's actions with children were deemed criminal violations of state law." Mr. Doe most likely could not sue the superintendent for the poor recommendation. However, school officials can lose qualified privilege if they act in bad faith or without regard for whether a statement is true.

In a recent case, an art teacher was deposed because a colleague had found out that the art teacher, upon request of the principal, had written a negative letter about her, even though she wasn't in the same department, did not serve as her supervisor, and did not see anything that she reported personally. This action potentially opened the art teacher who had written the letter up to a third-party hearsay libel suit, as well as the district, since the principal added the letter to the teacher's personnel file without informing the teacher or her union representatives. This letter further violated a collective bargaining agreement within the district. The teacher happened to exercise her right to request a copy of her personnel file from the central district without the administration's knowledge. This proved hurtful to the teacher, damaging to union and administrative parties, and led to legal action against the parties responsible for instigating and writing the document.

To avoid slander or libel suits, it is recommended that you only write or comment on observable behavior and attempt to avoid derogatory remarks. Even if you write a letter and the person waives his or her right to see it, if the person obtains a copy, you can be sued and held liable for what you wrote. This book recommends that if you can't write a positive letter of recommendation, then politely decline to write one at all. Here are some phrases to help you shy away from writing recommendations in which you may have reason to write something negative about the student, teacher, or fellow administrator. Sadly, because of the individual rights of employees on this issue, school districts often get sold a "bill of goods" with faulty administrators and teachers about whom former colleagues are unwilling to put negatives on paper.

I have some reservations about writing a letter. I think it better you ask someone else.

I am unable to judge your qualifications properly.

I don't write letters of recommendation.

I haven't observed you enough to comment.

I would be happy to speak to someone, but I will not be able to write a letter.

If you give me a copy of your résumé while working with us, I would be happy to verify facts from it.

I don't feel comfortable writing your letter. You need to ask another person. I hope you understand.

At this time, I am unable to write a letter on your behalf.

If you must document or write a letter in which you must mention poor performance, here are some phrases to help you:

In February 2008, Ms. Smith was not renewed. Further questions can be answered by our district lawyer. [Then don't comment any further.]

Due to an ongoing hearing involving Ms. Smith and the district, I am unable to discuss in depth the reasons behind contract nonrenewal.

Due to district policy, I can only confirm that Ms. Smith was not renewed for the 2010 academic year.

If you are evaluating a teacher who is not tenured for nonrenewal, it is advisable to write no comments at all. By writing comments you are opening your district up to grievances and appeals. Just bite your tongue and click the box that recommends a nonrenewal of the contract. Remember, no one owes a nontenured teacher an explanation. Don't comment, and the nonrenewal will stand on its own without other statements that may elicit a rebuttal.

If the teacher is tenured, it is highly suggested that you work with your district's lawyer to make sure that due process is afforded to the teacher. It is possible to remove tenured teachers; to do this, you just need to follow policy and procedures. Sometimes administrators think they can pressure a teacher to just leave, but their actions could be interpreted as retaliatory, vindictive, malicious, and not done in good faith. This again can open the district up to grievances and lawsuits.

Perfect Phrases for Evaluating Self-Performance and Licensure

Not all schools are the right match for every teacher or administrator. It is better to leave a difficult district for a better position when one becomes available. This is why you must keep self-performance evaluations and updated licensure. With each experience, you need to update your skills, and you need to remember that as an educator you will wear many hats. There are a number of different positions that you may want parents and administrators to know that you have held while serving as a teaching professional. In order for someone else to evaluate your performance, you must evaluate yourself. First sit down with a paper and pencil and figure out where you have been, where you are, and where you plan to go. Then start to write a résumé biography that can help you evaluate your performance as a teacher or administrator in the field of education. Here are some examples to get you started:

I have served during my tenure as an educator as a/ an [choose the terms that apply to your status: adjunct, advocate, aide, assistant principal, vice principal, dean of discipline, assistant superintendent, business manager, secretary to _____, coach, assistant coach, helper, chaperone, licensed teacher, long-term substitute teacher, paraprofessional, principal, headmaster, headmistress, retired teacher, substitute teacher, superintendent, union _____, _____ official, volunteer, PTA member, ESL teacher, SPED professional] . . .

I have held different positions in my teaching career. These have included . . .

Currently I am serving as the interim . . .

In the past, I have worked as a _____, and currently I am employed to . . .

My roles in education have consisted of wearing the following hats: . . .

To give you a little background about myself, I am/was [list your roles in education].

I have worked as a teacher/administrator/supervisor for _____ years.

For people to know and to evaluate you, you must show that you have a good education, have earned licensure, and have had relevant experience. In a competitive workplace, you must phrase your wording to show yourself to be the best potential employee during the evaluation process. These next phrases can help you to word your experiences:

During my tenure as an educator, I have been actively involved with . . .

During my university training, I was involved with . . .

I am a graduate of _____ program. I was awarded . . .

I am licensed in _____ areas with _____ status.

I've completed a successful student teaching experience with _____ .

I have _____ years of experience and expertise.

I have been the recipient of [list the awards, honors, grants, or scholarships].

I have presented talks at prestigious local/national/ international conferences such as . . .

I have published works in academic refereed publications such as . . .

I served on the following committees: . . .

I was elected to serve on the _____ executive board for . . .

In [year], I served as one of the _____ for the _____ conference.

My internship was with _____ on _____ street in [city, state] in the [season] of [year].

While at [school name], I taught . . . and served as . . .

My work was recognized by . . .

I published and presented at the _____ conference.

As an educator, districts and schools will want to evaluate the type of license you have. *Reciprocity* is a term that indicates a mutual or cooperative interchange between states to recognize each other's licenses. So if you want to teach outside of the state that licensed you,

you must apply to that district or state for reciprocity. In order for the district to consider your application or evaluate your teaching credentials, you would need to inform the district whether your license can transfer and under what conditions. Here are some phrases to use to ask for reciprocity to change your license to another state:

> *I would like to request license reciprocity.*

> *Currently, I am certified in the state of _____. It is my understanding that my state education licensure department has a reciprocal program with yours.*

> *I am seeking reciprocity.*

Revocation is a term that indicates that a teacher's license is suspended or terminated based on specific charges. Here are some phrases you can use if you face revocation but want to continue in a classroom so that districts can evaluate your ability to continue teaching:

> *My license was threatened for revocation after an alleged incident involving . . .*

> *My license has been revoked, but I am currently in the process of applying for its renewal.*

> *Revocation proceedings have not affected my license, so I would like you to evaluate my credentials.*

> *I would like to appeal the decision of revocation.*

> *I would like the documentation of charges leading to my revocation forwarded to you, as I believe that I was wrongly accused, as these documents will show. I am currently in the appeals process.*

How you are evaluated as a teacher or administrator depends on the certification or license that you possess from a governing body such as a board of education. For example, if you graduated from a teacher training program in Boston or Amherst, you would most likely be licensed by the Commonwealth of Massachusetts Department of Elementary and Secondary Education. Licensure is a serious process through which an educator is issued a professional license by the state. This license is based on educational training that meets the requirements of a governing board. Teachers in private and parochial schools aren't necessarily licensed, but teachers in public schools must be licensed unless they are given a special waiver for very specific reasons. If you are a teacher and you want to become a licensed educator in your state or one with reciprocity, here are some phrases to use to begin the process:

> *I would like to apply for licensure in [state].*

> *I am seeking to be licensed in [state] in the areas of _____.*

> *I have completed the requirements needed for licensure. Please accept this paperwork for my application to be licensed in the areas of . . .*

Technically, certification is different from licensure, as it is the educational process teachers undergo in order to get their teaching credential, or license to teach in a state. However, in practice the terms *certificate* and *license* and the terms *certification* and *licensure* are used interchangeably.

Here are some phrases that you can use during the certification process:

> *I am seeking certification in the areas of . . .*

> *I am enrolled in the following certification program: _____ for _____.*

> *I am certifiable. Currently, I request certification from _____ for _____.*

License renewal is when teachers reapply to keep their license active. Here are some phrases to use if you need to renew your certification or license:

> *I need to renew my license.*

> *I have completed the requirements for license renewal.*

Lapsed certification occurs when teachers don't reapply to keep their license active. For example, after retirement, many teachers don't renew their licenses with the state. However, after a few months of retirement they miss the classroom. Sometimes these teachers may be called back as long-term substitutes and run into the problem that their licenses have lapsed. These teachers need to work with the district to apply for waivers from the state board of education. Here are some phrases to use if you need to teach after your license has lapsed:

> *After retirement, I let my certification lapse. I would like to apply for a waiver to teach _____ .*

> *Due to an oversight, I allowed my certification to lapse. I need to reapply for my certification.*

> *My certification has lapsed. Therefore, I am requesting . . .*

A situation such as a suspended license can come up with both teachers and administrators. Suspension of a license suggests a period of time during which a person cannot use his or her professional license until a review board has investigated a claim and made a decision on whether to revoke or reissue the license. Here are some phrases you can use to explain why your license is suspended in an interview:

> *Due to an unforeseen circumstance, my teaching license has been suspended until _____ .*

*Although my license is suspended, it will be
reissued _____.*

*My license was temporarily suspended, but is expected to be
active again _____.*

Nonrenewal is a term that simply lets teachers know that a contract for the next year will not be forthcoming. This doesn't mean they were fired, but rather not issued a new contract for the following year. Here is a simple phrase to use when you were not renewed:

*I did not have tenure in the department, so I had to be the
colleague that was not renewed.*

*The principal was unable to renew my contract due to
financial constraints [or other reason].*

Phrasing the Differences in Licensing

Initial Licensing

Teachers are all different, and they go through different training programs and licensure. When describing your particular program or licensure, here are some phrases that you may want to use when you first graduate:

*Currently, I am enrolled in _____ teacher training
program.*

*My anticipated graduation from _____ teacher training
program will be on [date].*

*I have recently completed my student teaching and am
starting my initial licensure.*

*I was recently awarded initial licensure by the _____ and
have completed the teacher training program at _____.*

I am seeking licensure in the area(s) of . . . in [state/county/ ministry].

My new teacher's license allows me to . . . under the direction of . . .

Professional Licensing

Once you have started teaching, you will want to phrase your licensing differently. Here are some phrases that can be used to show you as a more midlevel professional:

I am licensed in the area(s) of: ESL (Pre-K–9), ESL (5–12), English (5–9), and English (9–12).

I am a certified teacher in [place].

The [state or country] Department of Education has issued me a/an [initial/primary/professional] license to teach [subject/ area/grade].

I was a graduate of the _____ teacher training program at _____.

I have been licensed for _____ years and have _____ years' teaching experience.

During my tenure as a teacher, I have been awarded [name award] under my license.

I am licensed to . . .

I am a certified teacher and have reciprocity with the following states/areas: . . .

I am a licensed educator who has [list accomplishments].

As a certified teacher, I have met the state requirements for renewal and have passed all tests and requirements for licensure.

Lapsed Licensure

If your certification has lapsed because you forgot to renew it or because you have retired, you may wish to use the following phrases:

I am a retired teacher with _____ years' experience. My license has lapsed, but I am still eligible for a state waiver.

I am currently in the renewal process for my license, which has lapsed due to . . .

Please note that I was licensed to teach . . . before my license lapsed.

My license needs to be reactivated in the area(s) of . . .

Potential Suspension or Revocation of a Certificate

During life, things will happen. For example, teachers get arrested and/or have other difficulties while applying for their licenses. Others have issues that may occur while teaching, such as driving under the influence of alcohol or drugs, morality issues, revocation complaints, or lawsuits that can suspend or hold up licensure. While applying for jobs, here are some key phrases that you may want to use to explain your situation:

I have spent the last _____ years of my life training to be a teacher in the _____ program. Unfortunately, and I deeply regret, I was involved in . . . that led to. . . . I am currently asking the state to reissue/issue/consider my application to teach _____.

I was a victim of a false allegation, which my lawyers have fought and won. Currently the state department of education is reissuing my license. As I have been exonerated, I would like to move on and begin a new teaching job in a new school. As court records show that I was not at fault, I ask that I be given a chance to interview with your district.

I was a teacher in the state of _____. I have now relocated to _____. I am seeking a teaching job with your district. [In this case, do not mention the issue unless asked.]

I am currently reapplying for my license. I expect that the state board will reissue it soon. [Don't list the reason—go for the interview and turn the negative into a positive.]

I deeply regret the pain and suffering I caused, but this was an accident. I have been through a treatment program and wish to go back to the classroom. I hope you will afford me a chance to teach with your school district as I was recognized as a superior classroom teacher.

Due to a personal matter, I took a period off from teaching. As the matter has passed, I wish to return to the classroom as a full-time/part-time teacher.

Not Licensed, but Teaching Experience

Private and parochial schools are not required to have licensed teachers. Oddly, many have more qualified teachers who, although they haven't gone through training programs, are highly educated and/or have work experience in the field in which they are teaching. Often retired public school teachers work in these types of schools without current licenses because it doesn't conflict with their retirement packages. If you are not licensed but you have had some teaching experience, here are some phrases that you may want to use:

I am not certified in [state/area/ministry], but I am certifiable.

I am not currently certified to teach in this state, but I believe that I could gain a waiver or become certifiable with the district's help.

I have taught _____ for _____ years. My certification has lapsed, but I am eligible for a waiver, if necessary.

My teaching experience has included [list—but don't mention that you are not certified].

Currently, I am seeking certification and am awaiting my [name state test] scores. I am seeking an entry-level teaching position in the area of _____ .

I have always been a natural born teacher. I have taught _____ for _____ . I don't hold a state certification, but I am looking into programs that offer licensure. I would like the opportunity to teach for your institution a course in my field of expertise, _____ .

No Teaching Experience and No Teaching License

It happens in certain economies that people are laid off and think about entering the field of teaching. Sometimes college graduates come out of school and decide they want to teach for a year. Other times, people want to change careers. Here are some phrases that can help you get teaching jobs:

During my career, I have served as . . . . I am looking to take my years of expertise and experience to help students in the classroom.

Although I have little/no classroom experience, I do have the expertise your district/school is looking for, as I have been [describe teaching-related experience].

As a recent graduate of _____ , I am seeking a teaching job with your school in the area(s) of . . .

After years of working in the _____ industry, I have decided to change careers and go into education. I am interested in teaching courses in the area(s) of . . .

I have taught in private/parochial schools for _____ years. I am seeking certification with the state currently in the _____ program. I would like to apply for the vacant position of _____.

I am seeking a teaching position that would allow me to . . .

I have completed a successful student teaching apprenticeship at _____.

Establishing Your Credibility as an Educator

It is important that you learn to comment on the facts in order to establish your authority as an educator in your assigned field. For example, it is important to describe what the students are learning from you. Here are some phrases that can help:

In my classes I make a conscience effort to . . . in order to help the children learn how to . . .

By the end of this course, your child should be able to . . .

During my _____ years of teaching, I have learned that it is essential for students to master the concept of . . .

I require students taking my class to . . .

This quarter/semester our class has covered the following material in the curriculum: . . .

We have been further practicing . . . , and I have seen satisfactory/unsatisfactory improvement by your child.

Your child has been studying . . . in my course. I have personally observed her . . . , and he or she has [excelled/ needs improvement] in the areas of . . .

The students have been exposed to . . . because I have used my expertise in the area of . . . to introduce them to the concepts of . . .

Please take a moment to glance over the curriculum I have been using with your child.

A teacher is a helper. You help your students in so many ways, and often you are not credited as an unsung hero. But in today's market, you must be able to stand out from the rest of the population when trying to find, maintain, or look for new opportunities of employment. Here are some phrases that you can use when you are an educator to explain how you have helped the students as a teacher, either alone or in collaboration with a peer:

. . . was instrumental in helping the students to . . .

. . . was both useful and helpful to our students trying to accomplish . . .

Aiding students by . . .

Assisted by . . .

Built in order to help a student . . .

Contributing to students' success were . . . and . . .

Demonstrated in the following practices, students were aided in . . .

Facilitated by . . . , the learners were assisted in . . .

Familiarized with . . . , the following individuals helped to . . .

Favoring, if not promoting, . . .

Helped to . . .

Performed under the guidance of . . .

Representing . . .

Solved and designed . . . to help students . . .

Students were aided . . .

Students were assisted through . . .

Students were the beneficiaries because . . .

Supplemental help was offered to . . . by . . .

Supporting and backing up . . . helped students who . . .

Supporting students through . . .

The students reaped the benefits of . . .

This enabled students to be assisted by . . . for . . .

Trained to . . . , the students can now . . .

Upholding our commitment to students, we aided them in . . .

Volunteers worked to help students . . .

We found . . . facilitative.

We found . . . to be helpful for students.

We found the supportive and comforting reassurance that students . . .

Working in conjunction with . . .

While interviewing, keep a positive attitude and never ask about money. Teachers are paid on a scale negotiated by unions. Everything should be about how much you love teaching children and how much learning means to you. Here are phrases you can use:

> *I went into the teaching profession because I love working with kids.*

> *I had a fantastic teacher, _____, who inspired me, and I hope to inspire others by . . .*

> *I love my field. My goal is to help kids be enamored with it as well.*

> *In school I was actively involved in . . . because I was mentored by _____. Now I hope I can take my skills and mentor students in . . .*

> *I want children to have chances like I was given. If it weren't for _____, I might not be here today. But here I am. I am here to give another child that same opportunity.*

Perfect Phrases for School Evaluation and Accreditation

Accreditation for schools began in response to serious concerns about the quality of childhood programs, the lack of uniform standards across the nation, and the lack of consensual definition of quality. Accreditation was initially proposed as a consistent strategy to help program personnel become involved in a process that would facilitate real and lasting improvements in the quality of the program. It was also intended to evaluate the quality of the program for the purpose of rating programs that demonstrated substantial compliance with criteria for a higher quality learning environment. To build consensus for the criteria and system to ensure validity, the process provided numerous systematic reviews and input from educators.

Now accreditation has been widely accepted, and parents often ask if their child is in a recognized accredited school system. Remember, just because a school received its accreditation in one review period doesn't guarantee its automatic renewal. The effect of the accreditation process is program quality. Issues that should be discussed and documented before an evaluation for accreditation to avoid problems during the preparation period include the following:

Collegiality of staff
Professional growth opportunities
Supervisor support and facilitative leadership
Clarity of policies and procedures
Reward systems for pay, job opportunity, advancement
Decision-making structures
Goal consensus in course programs and across the district
Task orientation regarding planning and efficiency
Innovativeness regarding adaptive change
Organizational climate
Current accreditation status
Ability to meet frameworks or standards set by the state or
    federal government
Sufficient faculty-to-student ratio
Staff turnover and qualifications
Programs available to students
Advisory councils and community resources
Relationship of parents, community, and students to program
    administration
Degree of parent altruism
Perception of the program by the state

By completing this process you will be able to better judge staff morale, the working condition of mission statements and goals, and the quality of current programs, and will show approval or disapproval of current programs in relationship to student retention and learning. Accreditation invests in public accountability, encourages transparency, and serves the public interest in meeting standards policy, and practice. As an administrator or teacher overseeing the process, especially in a private institution, you might want to use the following phrases when working on a school accreditation team:

Our schools will be up for accreditation on _____.

Most ministries of education have a very active committee on accreditation. These committees monitor the development of educational standards. I would like to take a moment to explain to the faculty how this affects our school.

Serving on these committees or answering to these groups requires you to carefully word your arguments for your mission statement, curriculum, and graduation standards.

We will be audited for academic credibility. It is necessary that we be exact with our . . .

Perfect Phrases to Introduce the Accreditation Process

The accreditation process should be explained to faculty and staff so that no one is excluded. It is essential that districts be able to justify their programs and curriculum to national boards that accredit schools. Here are phrases to meet a variety of situations that arise during accreditation periods:

We have convened a roundtable discussion among administrators, the accreditation team, and faculty on ways to preserve quality in our changing educational environment. We have concluded the following: . . .

As our institution has recognized . . . and . . . , we note that these policies and procedures, which address the responsibilities of the commission and its member institutions, are . . .

We welcome and wish to work with the recommendations made by the accreditation committee to improve the working standards of our institution. We ask faculty and staff to comply with this initiative by . . .

. . . are those documents and programs that refer specifically to the peer review process.

Note: The programs and services offered by member institutions, and administrative procedures of the commission, will subject us to . . .

We feel that this working document will help our school to . . .

As our faculty members know, our institution's handbooks, manuals, and other publications and its current policies provide . . .

_____ is a comprehensive set of documents describing all aspects of our accreditation protocol and related activities.

We ask for you to review these materials and to become more familiar with them during the accreditation process.

_____ describes the procedural requirements . . .

_____ will be used for our institutions and for the commission.

The guidelines provided for faculty are based on . . .

. . . are best practices as they provide advice to committee members.

. . . should be used for implementing the accreditation standards for our institution.

Faculty feedback is essential during the coming period leading up to the renewal of our accreditation.

Your feedback will help to improve our current academic practices and keep the commission in touch with . . .

Note: Constituent views on important issues affect policy development and our institution. Therefore we are asking faculty to . . .

The staff is responsible for . . .

Assigning chairs to teams that visit institutions and selecting the team members results in . . .

We are responsible to . . . , and, on that same note, we are responsible for . . .

At the current time, we do not know which individuals were drawn from a database of educators that the commission maintains . . .

We need your flexibility and cooperation to make our accreditation a success.

Faculties, departments, and grade levels are required to comply with the team during their visits. Please make yourself available to the team during their time with us.

Those who have not been a part of the accreditation process may have questions about the accreditation process. We wish to make the process transparent to all.

The team that will evaluate our programs will include individuals who have been recommended by the heads of institutions, colleagues who have themselves participated in the evaluation process, commission members, volunteers, and staff from the accreditation commission's committee. As a result our teams and committees will consist of . . .

The goal of this accreditation process is to ensure that the education provided by our institution meets acceptable levels of quality.

Accrediting agencies, which are private educational associations of regional or national scope, develop evaluation criteria and conduct peer evaluations to assess whether those criteria are met.

We are currently undergoing this process and . . .

Spearheading our accreditation teams will be . . . and . . .

As you know, accreditation involves nongovernmental entities as well as governmental agencies, therefore . . .

It is necessary for us to develop evaluation criteria and conduct peer evaluations to assess whether or not those criteria are met.

As higher education faculty members, you know that institutions and/or programs that request an agency's evaluation are required to . . .

To meet an agency's criteria, . . . must occur.

. . . are then accredited by that agency.

We have started this process and will be undergoing it for the period from _____ to _____.

The review process for accreditation is never easy; however, it is required by law if we wish to keep our . . .

If you foresee your inability to participate, you must contact us in writing with the details of your perceived exemption.

It is the accreditation team's duty to determine whether the standards used by our institution are comparable to the standards used to accredit equivalent institutions.

If you have further questions about the process we are about to undergo, please contact us for details.

Perfect Phrases to Describe Functions of Accreditation

This section offers educational administrators phrases to suggest best practices on behalf of the school or district to be used with evaluators. The phrases can be used with feedback groups, parent groups, evaluators, faculty subgroups, and for a wide audience of players who partake in the accreditation process. The phrases below serve as guidelines to help you phrase materials, programs, and meetings appropriately.

Verifying that an institution or program meets established standards is determined by . . .

_____ will be one of our set goals during the accreditation process.

To assist prospective students in identifying acceptable institutions, we have . . .

Assisting institutions in determining the acceptability of transfer credits will be judged on the following criteria: . . .

Helping to identify institutions and programs for the investment of public and private funds would be helpful if we are asked to explain future funding for . . .

We need to guard our institution against harmful internal and external pressure that may be expected in an audit. If you have ideas you wish to share with us on this topic, please contact _____ .

By creating goals for self-improvement of weaker programs, we have . . .

Involving the faculty and staff comprehensively in institutional evaluation and planning means that we must . . .

Establishing criteria for professional certification and licensure requires us to . . .

To upgrade courses offering such preparation, we must . . .

Providing one of several considerations used as a basis for determining eligibility for federal _____, we must consider . . .

The accrediting agency, in collaboration with educational institutions, establishes standards that . . .

The institution or program seeking accreditation prepares . . .

An in-depth self-evaluation study will . . .

_____ measures its performance against the standards established by the accrediting agency.

On-site evaluation means that . . .

A team selected by the accrediting agency visits the institution or program to determine firsthand if . . .

Upon being satisfied that the applicant meets its standards, the accrediting agency grants . . .

Accreditation or preaccreditation status states that . . .

Monitoring _____ results in . . .

The accrediting agency monitors will . . .

_____ is granted to verify that it continues to meet the agency's standards.

Reevaluation is needed.

The accrediting agency periodically reevaluates each institution or program that it lists to ascertain whether . . .

Perfect Phrases for Types of Accreditation

There are two basic types of educational accreditation: specialized, or programmatic, and institutional. Institutional accreditation normally applies to an entire institution. It normally will indicate that each of an institution's parts is contributing to the achievement of the institution's objectives. Here are some phrases that can be used to discuss the types of accreditation:

Although not necessarily all at the same level of quality, we . . .

The various commissions of the regional accrediting associations . . .

Specialized or programmatic accreditation normally applies to . . .

Programs, departments, or schools that are part of an institution are required to . . .

The accredited unit may be . . .

As large as a college or school within a university or as small as a curriculum within a discipline, the auditing accreditation board will . . .

Most of the specialized or programmatic accrediting agencies review . . .

_____ is an institution of educators that is accredited by one of the regional accrediting commissions.

However, certain accrediting agencies also accredit professional schools such as . . .

_____ and other specialized or vocational institutions of higher education are freestanding in their operations; this applies/does not apply to our school because . . .

Thus, an accrediting agency may also function in the capacity of . . .

We would like you to note that an institutional accrediting agency can . . . , but it cannot . . .

In addition, a number of specialized accrediting agencies have noted we've . . .

Note: The U.S. Department of Education does not have the authority to accredit . . .

Accrediting bodies for private or public elementary and secondary schools . . .

If an accrediting body that is recognized by the _____ also accredits elementary and secondary schools, the _____ recognition applies only to . . .

The agency's accreditation of _____ institutions means that . . .

Please understand that accreditation does not provide . . .

_____ is automatic acceptance by an institution of credit earned at another institution.

Acceptance of students or graduates is always the prerogative of the . . .

For these reasons, besides ascertaining the accredited status of a school or program, . . .

Students should take additional measures to determine, prior to enrollment, whether their educational goals will be met through attendance at a particular institution.

These measures should include inquiries to institutions to which transfer might be desired.

Many of you have questions about accreditation. For more than fifty years, there has been some type of nongovernmental coordinating agency for accreditation.

Whether or not you agree with the upcoming accreditation process, this body has existed primarily for the purpose of coordinating and improving the practice of accreditation.

_____, whose purpose is to foster and facilitate the role of accrediting agencies in promoting and ensuring the quality and diversity of American education, will . . .

_____ recognized, coordinated, and periodically reviewed the work of . . .

Until such time, we will be . . .

Perfect Phrases for Teacher Performance Evaluations

When writing teacher performance evaluations, you may want to describe a teacher's classroom management style. It is important to document observations of the teacher in order to accurately report what is happening in the classroom. It is better to be objective and to look for areas of strength and weakness. Here are some phrases that can be used in teacher evaluation reports:

Teacher takes prompt action.

Teacher manages time well.

Teacher brings out the best in learners.

Teacher effectively manages . . . .

Teacher knows how to stimulate learners.

Teacher strives to make work more meaningful.

Teacher challenges students to contribute more to their own learning.

Teacher fosters student autonomy.

Teacher maximizes learning instruction.

Teacher establishes realistic work demands.

Teacher effectively balances work flow.

Teacher offers peers professional development workshops.

Teacher uses consistent . . .

Teacher complies with state and federal regulations set forth for ELL/SPED.

Teacher effectively controls student behavior.

Teacher effectively deals with resistance.

Teacher copes with misunderstandings.

Teacher is a team player and contributes to the department.

Teacher is well informed in the subject area.

Teacher maintains strict compliance with . . .

Perfect Phrases for Supervisor and Team Leader Evaluations

As an educational administrator, you need to carefully balance your statements about those who serve under you. This type of evaluation should be honest, but very diplomatic. If you are asked to write evaluations for people who have acted in supervisory roles or as team leaders, you may want to put the title of the position first using a statement such as the following:

Supervisor monitors absenteeism.

Team leader is skilled in supervising difficult people.

Department head deals effectively with resistance.

Lead teacher reports all incidents promptly.

Here are some objective phrases for evaluating people who work in administrative roles that can accurately describe their ability to function as leaders in the school:

Follows all operating procedures closely.

Is an accurate evaluator.

Follows policies and procedures.

Understands and complies with local, state, and federal laws.

Applies rules and regulations fairly.

Maintains strict compliance with . . .

Manages the marginal performer.

Effectively deals with mistakes and errors.

Counsels faculty in best practices.

Has worked toward task-oriented team development.

Keeps members on task.

Works well with school district's administration.

Makes effective use of resources.

Maximizes the use of diverse talents of team members.

Establishes realistic schedules.

Meets timelines and deadlines.

Fosters school culture and meets district mission statements.

Handles special assignments and is open toward change.

Perfect Phrases for Professional Development and Committee Work Evaluations

Evaluating committee members can be awkward. In many cases, the members under contract are doing work on a voluntary basis because the hours expected are never covered. As the team leader of committees, you often have to rely on people's goodwill. But you must also make sure that everyone is pulling his or her weight on the project. When evaluating committee work, you want to create a rubric that addresses the following areas, depending on the task assigned:

- Ability to break down work into phases
- Ability to follow safety procedures
- Ability to communicate to team members clear goals and deadlines
- Ability to meet expectations
- Ability to meet and set goals
- Ability to handle personal problems with professional life
- Ability to meet and set goals
- Ability to meet deadlines
- Professional appearance, self-esteem, and confidence
- Attitude toward the work and the team and commitment to the project
- Communication skills (oral and/or written)
- Conflict resolution and ability to de-escalate issues
- Contribution to the team
- Creativity and innovation

- Decision-making ability
- Efficient use of time
- Empowerment of committee members
- Individual contribution and team contribution
- Instruments used to measure improvement and ability to follow directions
- Leadership skills and ability to work with the committee chairperson
- Loyalty to the school or institution in terms of effort offered toward the committee
- Motivation of others or self-motivation
- Negotiation skills and ability to compromise during the process
- Openness to change
- Overall production
- People skills and the use of diplomacy and tact
- Problem solving within given time constraints
- Project management style
- Punctuality
- Teamwork
- Technical skill development and ability to use different forms of creative media
- Use of common sense and good judgment

Perfect Phrases for Classroom Observation Evaluations

By contract, all districts perform classroom observations. It is an area that people don't always feel comfortable addressing because teachers feel the administrator's visit may be biased, not a realistic reflection of what happens in their classroom every day, or intrusive. It is not the observation itself that upsets teachers. It is the meeting afterward that stresses educators out because they feel they are at the mercy of one person's opinion. When this is coupled with the fact the educators often find it difficult to accept feedback or criticism, it can cause tension. What teachers forget is that people around the world in the workplace are all judged and evaluated based on performance. The difference between educators and the average worker is that we have a little more protection than our colleagues in the business world.

Over the years, when observing veteran teachers, I have used self-evaluation methods that ask the teacher to meet with me in advance of the observed lesson to discuss what they want to do in the classroom. Next, I let them teach the lesson without me in the room. After the class, I meet with them and ask, "If you could do it again before I come in to watch, what might you change about the lesson? Where did it work or fail?" I have found that the teachers are more critical of themselves than I would be. They also were forced to think about their teaching strategies and to self-reflect on their own lesson. It also promotes a very good working relationship between the teachers and me because it fosters professional communication. However, by contract administrators may have to go into the classroom and observe teachers. If so, the administrator should follow these simple rules:

- Always be frequent and sincere with your feedback.
- Make feedback fast, helpful, and corrective.
- Be empathetic and sensitive to the teachers' feelings.
- Be empathetic to any nervousness of the person being observed.

Phrases that you might want to use to ease a teacher into constructive feedback sessions after observing a lesson include the following:

Before we begin, do you have any thoughts on how you would like to proceed?

Can you share with me areas where you might be having difficulty?

Feedback can be presented in a multitude of ways, and as your supervisor it is my responsibility to help establish a more productive learning environment.

How would you like to receive helpful and constructive feedback from me?

I feel as if we are getting off on the wrong foot. I do not intend this as a personal attack, but you aren't currently compliant with all of the educational guidelines.

I do not want you to feel criticized, but I need to find a way to give you feedback. What suggestions can you offer me on the best way to do this?

I understand that this might be difficult for you, but I care about your learning how to . . . correctly.

I want to document performance achievements, but I also have to note areas for future improvement.

I want to give you feedback in a timely manner. Can you set up an appointment with me?

Let's meet as soon as possible to discuss a more proactive approach to the performance problem of . . .

May I suggest the option of . . . ?

Perhaps we can discuss your observation tomorrow morning.

This may not apply to you, but I am going to share it with you anyway.

What makes you the most comfortable when receiving feedback?

Some administrators have no backbone and try to find the positive where it doesn't exist, while others can lack tact and be offensive with their comments and feedback. Let's look at some real sample situations that I have seen happen in schools.

Case One: You sit in the back of the room to do an observation, and the teacher points you out to the class. The teacher insists you participate in the lesson, gives you praise, and keeps involving you instead of letting you simply observe. What do you say or do?

You could think, "Cut it out," but you dare not say it. Instead, in this case it is best to politely excuse yourself and meet with the teacher later. During the conference, explain that involving you in the lesson prevents you from observing the teacher's usual interaction with the students and that another observation will need to be done in place of the one that went askew.

Case Two: You are part of an old-boy network who likes to cover up incidents so they don't go public. You notice something inappropriate with a teacher who is well connected. As the administrator, you may try to explain it away, but the community and others will know. It won't remain secret for long, and if the issue is pushed, you may be wrapped up in a legal case or worse if you knew and didn't act.

Case Three: You enter the room to do the observation, and it is obvious that the teacher is repeating a lesson he or she has already done with the students, so that it looks like the students are putting on a production for your benefit. You may be tempted to offer the teacher an Oscar for the best performance in a staged classroom, but again you cannot do this. You may instead want to ask the students if they have studied this material previously, because they will tell on the teacher. It may be necessary to curtail the observation and return to perform a new observation on another date, within the guidelines of the contract or collective bargaining agreement.

While performing observations, you must think about what you are saying and how honest you want to be. Also remember that observations become a part of the teacher's personnel file, which makes what you say and how you say it very important! Sometimes a simple word will haunt a person, and performance will deteriorate. Instead of seeing the one hundred times it went right, we can sometimes document the one time it didn't. This can upset the person receiving the evaluation, so it is important to put things into perspective.

During the process of evaluation you should preempt problems by identifying obstacles to an employee's performance. For example, if a teacher is being observed and the learners don't bring materials to class, is it the teacher's fault? Should the learners' behaviors affect the teacher's evaluation? I have often thought of this as the "student goes lame" principle. You choose a certain class for an observation, and on the day of the observation that class has for whatever reason a high rate of absences, missing work, or forgotten materials and lacks a true reflection of participation. The students either overcompensate or sit like zombies behind their desks until the bell rings, and of course there will always be the one student who has "comments" to make because he or she thinks the evaluation process is a game. This is why observations can be ineffective measures of a teacher's ability. As a matter of fact, observations can be the least reliable of all the measurement tools, if done incorrectly. There are many elements to the observation process. For example, when an administrator, department head, or team leader first observes the class, the person should check for the following:

- A lesson plan
- A board space divided into three areas for information to be learned, information that will come up in class, and/or homework assignments
- Teacher techniques when students enter or leave the classroom
- Teacher's ability to work with disruptions
- Student background
- Level, student ability, and time of the class
- Student-to-teacher ratio
- Student-to-teacher and student-to-student interaction patterns
- Modeling of materials

- Accuracy of information provided to students
- Number of times the teacher stops or doesn't have contingencies if something goes awry
- Techniques the teacher uses to make the materials easier to learn
- The tension level in the room
- How the teacher overcomes obstacles presented by students
- The teacher's perspective on the class he or she is teaching

Next, look at the teacher's ability to communicate information to the learners in the classroom. Note whether or not the teacher does the following:

- Demonstrates an appropriate attention span
- Uses good verbal skills
- Uses good grammar
- Uses good written communication
- Speaks clearly
- Gives clear directions and instructions
- Is able to answer student questions
- Understands subject materials
- Avoids coming across as defensive or threatened
- Demonstrates good classroom management
- Stays on topic during a class
- Uses appropriate humor
- Avoids being too casual with students
- Repeats points appropriately
- Makes enough accommodations to meet the needs of special education learners
- Commits to a decisive plan of action in the lesson
- Has good classroom control without raising voice
- Is punctual in starting and stopping activities
- Makes appropriate decisions
- Avoids micromanaging students

- Is not intimidated by students
- Shows delegation skills
- Is consistent in his or her methods
- Refrains from sarcasm
- Has positive interactions with learners
- Is helpful to students
- Displays nonprejudicial behavior
- Maintains a nonstressful classroom environment
- Treats students fairly
- Presents professional lessons
- Welcomes student feedback
- Shows enthusiasm toward the subject
- Provides accurate information
- Suggests ideas to further facilitate learning
- Is sensitive to students' needs

When the teacher is evaluating students, watch for how the instructor words his or her praise. Sometimes teachers can be condescending and use remarks that are offensive to students and impede learning. As the administrative leader, it is your job to train the teachers to avoid derogatory comments and use phrases that are more objective and neutral. Some teachers have not learned how to put comments in writing and will write the way they talk. Here are some example phrases you can use with teachers to help them:

Accepts responsibility

Accurately spells weekly lists

Adjusts to differences in materials

Applies language mechanics

Applies spelling skills to everyday work

Applies writing process

Asks appropriate questions

Beginning to learn how to . . .

Can answer questions appropriately

Can complete with adult supervision

Can complete with modifications

Completes classwork on time

Completes homework on time

Completes work most of the time

Controls talking

Courteous and respectful to others

Creates original work and projects that reflect the materials being learned

Demonstrates an interest in independent reading

Demonstrates an understanding of what is read

Demonstrates and organizes skills

Demonstrates effort

Edits and revises work

Exhibits self-control

Focuses and sustains attention

Follows directions

Forms letters correctly

Grade reflects specialized instruction

Interprets written questions

Knows addition facts

Knows division facts

Knows multiplication facts

Knows subtraction facts

Listen to learn and learn to listen

Listens with understanding

Makes good use of self-directed time

Needs more practice copying . . .

Needs penmanship improvement

Needs to finish assignments

Needs to further practice printing/cursive letters

Needs to practice focusing on the teacher without being distracted

Needs to turn in assignments in a timely manner

Observes school rules

Oral reading and fluency

Raises hand when seeking an answer to a question

Shows promise in the area of . . .

Stays on task for appropriate periods of time

Takes care of property and materials

Is consistent in . . .

Understands concepts

Uses meaning in context

Uses phonics

Uses problem-solving strategies

Uses whole language

Works cooperatively in groups

Works well independently

Works well with help from an aide

Works without disturbing others

Writes neatly

Perfect Phrases for Lesson Plan Evaluations

Lesson plan evaluation is essential because it is the method that the teacher uses to convey the curriculum. Lessons should be organized and consistent with district and state goals. When a lesson plan is to be evaluated by a third party, it should justify the materials being taught. For example, teachers might say the following:

I will justify the grading process by . . .

I will relate to the students the grading criteria.

In order to evaluate their work, students will describe . . .

In order to validate students' progress, I will offer a pretest and posttest to the lesson.

It will be important to contrast student work by . . .

The biggest question that will then be asked is how the teacher will get students to meet the aims and objectives set forth in the lesson plan. For evaluative purposes you may want to suggest different methods that a student might use to meet the aim or objective. Here are some sample phrases:

Playing devil's advocate, groups will argue . . .

Students will be asked to self-critique . . .

Students will be evaluated on . . .

Students will decide whether or not . . .

Students will explain . . .

Students will interpret their evaluations . . .

Students will use a chart to discriminate . . .

The grade will be concluded by . . .

Students will be graded in a summarized form based upon . . .

Students will be required to standardize their work to MLA or APA formats.

The work will be assessed by a rubric, which will be devised by . . .

In the evaluation of the lesson plan, if you are critiquing the teacher's aims and objectives, you might want to look for the following items and use these phrases:

Clearly identifies the target audience

Effectively elicits students' prior knowledge

Effectively supports students' efforts to learn new . . .

Establishes a specific purpose/focus for . . . that is appropriate and is explicitly stated to students

Uses at least one instructional . . . strategy

Uses proper materials and follows appropriate procedures

Incorporates instructional theories and/or models

Uses a wide range of age-appropriate activities to increase student interaction

Incorporates a time frame of presentation

Lesson and materials used are age and ability appropriate for learners

Perfect Phrases for Department and Leadership Evaluations

Often administrators and teachers have to evaluate departments within a school. They have to look at how the department functions as a team, because dissent from just one member can bring destruction and prevent progress. Department members can work against their supervisor in deceitful ways, or they can work with their supervisor to create a more positive environment on behalf of children. Here are some phrases to consider using when thinking about the role the team has played in creating a working department:

[Name] has contributed to the team by . . .

The team created . . . , and the project was successful.

The team worked together for the greater good of the school and its students.

The team prepared timely and excellent quality reports.

The team demonstrated competing priorities.

The team used/didn't use analytical methods.

The team needs to consider broader implications.

The team welcomed challenges as opportunities to overcome problems or issues.

The team incorporated technology-based education.

The team used its competitive edge to . . .

The team worked/did not work within budgetary constraints.

The team found cost reductions that saved the district money.

The team gave an effective presentation.

The team was persuasive in its arguments.

The team was productive.

The team maintained an unusually high output.

The team developed creative and cost-effective solutions.

The team accepted the project with enthusiasm.

The team kept the project on target and met deadlines.

The team sought input from multiple sources.

The team encouraged the maximum contribution from each member.

The team helped teachers to excel.

The team members showed leadership qualities.

The team has strong communication skills and presented the school in a positive light.

The team demonstrated tact and diplomacy.

The team welcomed new members.

The team set clear goals and objectives.

The team established realistic timelines.

The team showed a spirited effort.

The team maximized its diverse talent.

The team resolved conflicts.

The team encouraged full participation from all of its members.

The team worked together with the committee chairperson to produce . . .

The team remained task-oriented.

The team provided management with periodic reports.

The team drew on the strengths of its members.

The team worked to develop an organizational culture that fosters a more productive environment.

Perfect Phrases for Teacher Improvement Plan Evaluations

First it is important to recognize any problem areas. If you are evaluating a teacher and you want to show areas for improvement, here are some phrases you can use in your reports:

The teacher needs to work on creating a more language-rich classroom to engage students' interest and imagination.

Teacher must improve upon his or her teaching methods to make students more proficient readers.

The instructor needs to focus on making students more independent learners.

The teacher could incorporate research into each week's lessons.

The teacher should consider reading to the class.

In order to pace instructions so that learning is achieved and skills are practiced, it is suggested that the teacher . . .

To help students demonstrate a desired learning behavior, it is recommended that the teacher . . .

Instructor should increase emphasis on attitude as well as knowledge.

Instructor should observe and monitor groups more frequently.

Teacher should maximize students' time on task by simplifying and creating standardized procedures so that time is spent on the learning activity rather than on directions.

It is suggested that the teacher give examples of related words and their spellings after the key word is learned.

Teacher needs improvement in modeling information.

Teacher needs to emphasize mental independence rather than mental acceptance.

Teacher should increase use of direct instruction.

In order to allow for freedom in thinking, teacher needs to . . .

Teacher should choose activities that practice reading high-frequency words.

Teacher should increase focus on accuracy.

Teacher might want to consider computer-based programs for more individualized practice and reinforcement.

Teacher needs to correct answers to reinforce the use of . . .

Teacher should encourage guessing as a way to help students connect with materials.

Teacher needs to give both oral and written directions.

Teacher needs to help students track success using different strategies to accomplish a frequent task or assignment.

Teacher needs to implement . . .

Teacher needs to improve pacing of materials.

Teacher needs to improve the environment to maximize student engagement in the lesson.

Teacher needs to keep the language simple, number the steps, and use flowcharts to show . . .

Teacher needs to permit students to draw . . .

Teacher needs to post the directions on the board in order to keep students on track.

Teacher needs to provide more informative feedback.

Teacher needs to remind students of key words and their spellings.

Teacher needs to scan response more often.

Teacher needs to track individual students' learning.

Teacher needs to use more group response methods.

Teacher should incorporate more graphic organizers to show similarities and differences.

Teacher should encourage students to underline or color code the key elements.

Teacher should use a visual thesaurus to show word relations.

Teacher needs to present information at a slower pace.

Teacher needs to match the modality of instruction to the students by using . . .

Teacher should encourage creativity rather than conformity.

Teacher should emphasize the role of self-determination rather than authority in teaching respect for others.

Teacher should relate instruction to the lifestyle of the students to make it less academic.

The classroom teacher should decrease the emphasis on the textbook.

The classroom teacher should emphasize active rather than passive learning.

The course's instructor should place more emphasis on original thought.

The instructor needs to keep the active learning level high for all students.

The instructor needs to work on teaching more decoding skills, high-frequency words, and other aspects of the language, such as . . .

The lesson needs more advanced organizers.

The teacher needs to encourage students' individuality.

The teacher needs to review the IEP plans of students and tailor lessons accordingly.

The teacher needs to use more cues or prompts to guide students' work.

The teacher needs to work on giving feedback in a more neutral tone.

The teacher should make more connections between the materials to help students learn the information.

The teacher should decrease use of routine to promote student initiative.

The teaching objectives need to be made more utilitarian.

The use of concept mapping to help students organize what they know about a concept is recommended for this instructor.

To provide immediate and clear feedback, it is suggested that the teacher . . .

Using error analysis as a basis for planning instruction and practice activities, the district suggests that the teacher . . .

We recommend that the teacher use structured or guided practice to gradually move the students from fully supported to fully independent work.

Perfect Phrases for Underperforming and Needs Improvement Evaluations

Great teachers need little guidance, but for the rest feedback is essential. Many schools are underperforming because teachers are not teaching or holding students accountable. Teachers are not correcting homework or giving feedback promptly. Time is wasted in the classroom. When teachers underperform, students underperform, and as a result your school as a whole underperforms. If you want to make sure you are offering teachers due process, chances for improvement, or a contract the following year based on improvement, you need to let them know what they need to improve upon in the classroom. Here are phrases for documenting underperforming teachers:

The teacher has little classroom control.

The teacher uses only the textbook in presenting lessons.

The teacher does not participate in after-school activities.

The teacher does not follow policies and procedures.

The teacher is not willing to work with continuous improvement methods.

Teacher has not shown a plan of improvement.

Teacher has violated the contract by . . .

Teacher's class disturbs the learning environment in other classrooms.

Teacher makes paperwork errors.

Teacher is late with paperwork.

Teacher doesn't keep up-to-date records.

Teacher does not reply to requests for information.

Teacher's grading policies are not consistent.

Teacher is not recommended for contract renewal.

Teacher is insubordinate and refused to . . . when requested.

Teacher is unwilling to . . .

Teacher needs constant direction. For example, . . .

Teacher does not attend team meetings.

Teacher does not keep information confidential.

Teacher refuses to take on new assignments.

Parents have registered complaints about the teacher.

Teacher doesn't check his or her mail.

Teacher doesn't take daily attendance.

Teacher speaks ill of students in public places like the faculty room.

Teacher expresses constant negative views during staff meetings.

Teacher does union business on teaching time.

Teacher's grading practices have been called into question by . . .

Teacher undermines the administration or students by . . .

Teacher is repeatedly late for school.

Teacher's actions are in violation of . . .

The teacher has endangered the health, welfare, or safety of students by . . .

Chapter 5

Union Issues

Local school boards have the legal authority to hire and fire teachers. Most local school committees have written contracts with their teachers. These boards have discretion in deciding employment contracts as long as they do not violate an individual's constitutional or statutory rights.

Local school boards are supposed to hire teachers who already have certification first, and then hire people with waivers or who are working on their certification. But as we all know, that doesn't always hold true, because it is cheaper for a district to hire a new teacher than one who will come in on a different salary scale. Unfortunately, teachers with the most experience are discriminated against in district employment simply because collective bargaining contracts have made them too expensive to hire.

Contracts vary from district to district. There is no such thing as a federal contract for all teachers across the United States. Some school districts have more detailed contracts that result from collective bargaining negotiations. The union becomes the bargaining agent for the teachers with the school committee. The union will define the terms and conditions of employment including wages, salaries, benefits, and pay scales. It may also create stipulations that regulate class size. If a problem needs to be resolved it will depend on the language and context of the contract and may depend on state or federal laws to clarify issues of concern. However, it is important to remember that the contract is not binding until it is approved by the school board or committee.

The courts determined long ago that teachers have the right to form unions—thanks to the teachers from Norwalk, Connecticut, who challenged their board of education in court. But with unions come negotiations. Interestingly, a contract doesn't have to be in writing, and unilateral contracts that describe tenure and dismissal policies can be put in place for teachers. The contract will state how long it is in effect, but many times districts work without a contract. These periods are often referred to as "work to rule." Sometimes labor relation boards involve themselves in the process on behalf of the educators since they are public employees—for example, if an administrator or district representative attempts to influence contractual negotiations between a union and a school committee. School committees working with collective bargaining agreements cannot bypass the union and make salary agreements with individual teachers.

Teachers who belong to unions are not allowed to legally strike. But more recently, some states have passed laws that allow teachers to participate in "limited strikes" after the union has complied with the state's procedures for impasse resolution and notified the school board. Teachers who engage in a strike illegally may have wages deducted; lose dues deductions; be dismissed, suspended, or demoted; have their contract suspended; and may be held liable in some state courts for costs suffered as a result of the strike by school districts. Teachers may also be sued by students for emotional distress and being deprived of an education if the educators illegally strike. It is important to note that although charter schools are public schools, they are not necessarily part of a union and may be separate from a district, leaving teachers of such institutions unprotected.

Teachers do not have the constitutional right to bargain with school boards as individuals. Every collective bargaining contract is different depending on the teachers' needs in that district. However, if you are an administrator who may serve on the union, there are some basic components of the contract that you should be aware of:

- A preamble that identifies the parties and the period of the contract
- A recognition clause that identifies the unions and associations, such as the Pittsfield Teacher's Union and the Massachusetts Teachers' Association, and states who is the exclusive representative of each party
- A maintenance clause that provides no change in the terms and explains the conditions
- A grievance procedure that describes the steps to be followed if a grievance is filed (A grievance is a claim by the teacher that the union contract has been violated. This is why it is important for all parties to have a copy of the union contract.)
- A teachers' rights clause stating the right to organize that prevents retaliation or discrimination against union members
- A teachers' organization rights clause that outlines rights to communicate with other members
- A representation clause that describes the procedure to be followed if the school board or an employee organization wants to challenge the role of the union as the exclusive bargaining agent
- A management rights clause that affirms the rights of the school committee
- Terms of agreement that describe the specifics of the contract provisions

The union and school committee cannot just make up contract terms to argue about for the sake of arguing. Instead they must follow state laws. When laws aren't specific, then issues can be bargained. For example, if you are a teacher in Massachusetts, the length of the school calendar is mandated, but the number of pupils in your class can be bargained. Unions can also bargain on student discipline procedures.

Both the union and the school committee are supposed to bargain in good faith. For example, if a principal took it upon himself or herself at a departmental meeting to attempt to influence the teachers' voting to pass a contract, he or she could be brought up on ethics charges by a labor board. A recent case in Massachusetts that involved a principal's interference in the collective bargaining process led to the superintendent's district letter of reprimand being printed on the entire back page of a newspaper. The document was paid for by the teachers' union as a reminder to administrators and districts of what constitutes good faith and ethical bargaining. Remember that during the collective bargaining process the teachers' union and school board will draft proposals and there will be exchanges and negotiations that are both positive and negative. Unions are under no obligation to reach agreements with school boards, and vice versa.

Perfect Phrases for Negotiating Contracts

Negotiation between unions and school committees involves a process of give-and-take, and there are some deliberate steps you can take to effectively manage this debate, using principles from psychology. Your aim is to get people to do what you want them to do. The following advice can make your wording more effective:

- Personalize your statements by using the pronoun *I* to show the issue is really affecting you. Or, when you wish to emphasize the strength of your ideas, use the collective *we* in your statements.
- Use the active voice and avoid the passive to simplify your statements.
- Talk in the conditional tenses, because then you aren't threatening with statements, but instead looking at what might happen *if* something were to occur.

- Don't make comments on the passing time because people will focus on that instead of what you are saying.
- Use firm but intimate body language. Don't cross your arms or point, and speak with open palms and gestures that indicate openness to what others are saying.
- Speak of *problems* when something you oppose is suggested, but of *challenges* when you suggest something. It will psychologically imply that the obstacles are greater for the suggestion you oppose.
- Always adopt a firm but comfortable stance on issues. Drop the emotion and keep explaining your stance rationally. Like the directions on a shampoo bottle, repeat when necessary.
- Stand your ground without being inflexible. If people smell weakness they will eat you alive, and if they see that you have dug your heels in they won't bother giving you valuable options to work with, so find a happy medium.
- Remember teachers have the NEA and other huge organizations backing them, so remember to pick the battles you want to fight in order to win the war.
- Dress and act like a professional if you want to be treated like one at the table.
- Use proper diction, pronunciation, and grammar. Don't use street language, vulgarities, slang terms, or jargon in bargaining meetings.
- Pick a person who doesn't take things personally to speak for your view in case the other side attacks the individual instead of the issue.
- Make sure you use media to your advantage by presenting them with the information that supports your recommendations. You don't have to divulge everything.
- Understand that you will survive mistakes and that no matter how badly the day may go in the negotiations, the sun will still rise tomorrow. Keep up a positive, can-do attitude.

- Support your statements with facts and figures because people rely on numbers and quantitative data.

As one who has filed and won grievances against administrators, I have found that many things could have been avoided had the administrators put their pride aside and simply said, "Sorry for the misunderstanding. I had a bad day." But many administrators consider saying the three simple words "I am sorry" to be a weakness, and so a mountain is made from a molehill as things begin to escalate on both sides. The first piece of advice in dealing with potential grievances is that you have to understand that there will be give-and-take, battles won and lost, and flexibility is key. This means that in order to have a positive outcome, you will need to make the most of your assets.

This means knowing what people are likely to be willing to agree to from instinct. If you push the limits and corner people, like a tiger, they will come pouncing out at you and ferociously attack. If you lie or misrepresent issues, people who work for ethical reasons will fight to win moral grounding at any cost. If you work with people who are shallow, you know where they can be bought out or will cave, but prepare yourself for the fighter: the teachers or administrators who are like cockroaches, emerging from the depths triumphant despite how many times you try to squash them!

The goal is to negotiate without giving in, and as the bestseller reads in its title, you want to "get to yes" with the person. Here are some perfect phrases to help you do so:

Would you be open to meeting with a third party for resolution?

What profit is in it for us to fight and waste energy on this topic that in the bigger picture has little significance?

I would prefer not to bargain over positions but rather to discuss where we aren't seeing eye to eye.

I think we are not separating the people from the problem, so it is causing contention.

Do you mind if we focus on interests instead of positions?

Do you feel there is any way to solve our dispute that would give us both mutual gain?

Do you mind if we discuss each other's perceptions on this issue?

I recognize and understand your emotions, but do you think you could look at . . . with a more objective outlook?

I would like to look forward, not back. So, where do you think is a midpoint from which to begin?

What might be done to resolve this conflict?

I want to hear what you have to say. I also want you to hear what I have to say.

We clearly have a difference in opinion. At this point, is it fair to say we agree to disagree?

I feel we are bringing a more stressful situation upon ourselves with our inability to reach resolution. Do you agree?

What are you willing to and not willing to concede in these talks?

Perfect Phrases for Resolving Contract Disputes

As stated earlier, a contract doesn't have to be in writing, and an oral contract that has met legal requirements may be legally binding. A contract is not binding for a teacher or an administrator until the school board approves it. Because school boards act as public bodies, they cannot ratify a contract without taking official action. Contracts don't have to be detailed and are often vague. Many are vague to allow for ambiguity and interpretation on both sides, which becomes important in the grievance process. The contract is actually completed once the parties follow five steps:

1. There is a meeting of the two parties.
2. Valid considerations are taken and issues negotiated.
3. Legal subject matter is written.
4. Competent parties approve it.
5. Contract terms are further defined through the resolution process.

Contract disputes arise in a variety of contexts, and the resolution can depend on the language and specifics of the particular collective bargaining agreement or contract. Teachers can work without a contract but may have difficulty getting back money or collecting money. Teachers can break a contract, but they can also be sued for breaching the contract. A teacher who doesn't abide by the terms of the contract may also breach it. If you breach a contract as a teacher or administrator, the court can make you pay damages to the school district. Just as a teacher can sue a district for lost wages if the district breaches the contract, a district can sue a teacher for similar results. If you are a teacher who breaches the contract, you may have to pay the salary difference between the cost to actually hire you and the new salary cost for the instructor, human resource costs, and perhaps legal fees. Be aware that some collective agreements have liquidated damage clauses, as well as punishments for a teacher who breaches the contract.

In some states the district can seek revocation of your teaching license for breaking the contract by failing to comply with the contractual agreements. Contracts can also end under what is known as the impossibility of performance. This topic is controversial. For example, if a physical education teacher weighs 450 pounds and is a chain smoker, can he or she still perform his or her duties as an educator in that specific field? It is a great debate amongst all parties, and other factors such as age, race, gender and past precedence are considered. It is advisable to consult your state laws and local board policies to find out what affects you and your contract.

Because they can have such serious consequences for schools, districts, and teachers, phrases for contracts should not be drawn up by you as the administrator, no matter how tempting, but by legal representatives who will look out for your district's best interests. Once a contract is in effect, however, it may be your responsibility to assist in negotiations to resolve contract disputes or grievances.

Negotiating is an art form. If you are not a negotiator, I suggest you go to a flea market, select an item you want that seems highly overpriced, and begin the bargaining process with the owner. Instantly, you will become a negotiator, because you won't be willing to pay what the seller is asking and will only purchase the item if you and the seller can reach mutually acceptable terms. When negotiating you need to use phrases such as the following that suggest what you want to do to further the resolution:

Discuss . . .

Talk over some issues

Confer with . . . about what should be done

Consult those with more expertise or experience

Parley the messages to . . . for further opinion

Agree to disagree at the moment

Cooperate and/or collaborate with . . .

Hope that we can reach a deal that we both find acceptable

In negotiating the dispute, you want to use phrases that suggest you are willing to be flexible. Here are some examples that might prove useful:

Would you mind a contingent agreement?

I hope to work with you in good faith.

What arbitrary outcome would you like to see?

Let's see what items we can agree upon, so we can move negotiations along.

Perfect Phrases for Grievance Procedures

Not every complaint a teacher or administrator makes is a grievance! A grievance is a formal allegation that the school has not complied with the union contract. It states what rules or procedures have been misinterpreted, misapplied, or violated; who is responsible; and what should be done to correct the problem. If you believe you can grieve an issue, contact your union representative, who will go over the issues and contract with you to see if you have a legitimate case.

The first step is an informal grievance procedure that allows the two parties to try to work the problem out before it goes public. Teachers can usually expect administrators to turn them down at stage one.

The second step usually involves the superintendent of a district or some other official. Again you can pretty much expect to get turned down at level two, because the district doesn't want to admit fault, and the administrator wants to be perceived as backing his or her team of administrators. These administrators may also play a part in this person's job or contract renewal.

The third step is where the action is taken, and usually the grievance is heard by the school committee, which should be made up of neutral parties that have to think in the best interests of the district

Some districts may opt for mediation or a third-party resolution to solve the issue.

The fourth step is arbitration. Arbitration happens if an agreement has not been mediated to resolve the situation. Arbitrators' decisions are usually final and often, but not always, in favor of the faculty member. In certain instances, teachers can stop the grievance procedure and sue under state statutes such as the state's "whistle-blower statute" if one is in place, especially if the teacher claims to be protecting the health, welfare, and safety of children. Here are some perfect phrases that can be used in grievance procedures:

The contract has been violated.

I would like to request help from my union representative.

As per the collective bargaining agreement, I would like to grieve . . .

According to . . . in the teacher or administrator's contract, the following sections have been violated: . . .

I would like to waive the process and hire private litigators.

I would like to appeal the grievance to the next step.

I would like to request that a formal grievance be filed.

I would like to have materials expunged from my personnel file.

Chapter 6

Curriculum and Standardized Testing

This section is intended to help principals and other administrators with oral and written communication related to curriculum and standardized testing. If a parent or teachers' group wants to find the weak points in a district, they are most likely going to start in these areas. Therefore, it is important that you have formal policies, objectives, and reasoning in place to defend why and what you are teaching within the district.

Perfect Phrases for Course Descriptions

It is important to be able to describe how your staff teaches a particular course. Parents may want to know how your school approaches teaching. Here are some phrases to best describe what students learned and how your school's philosophy applies to the courses:

This is our first year offering this course in _____.

We have designed the course so that it can . . .

Our courses are mirrored to meet state guidelines and standards. For example, please note . . .

Our programs were designed to serve . . .

To perfect our programs, we constantly seek feedback.

We believe that just "good enough" is never good enough for our students.

The school's educational philosophy is based upon . . . , so it is only natural that our programs are based upon . . .

We strive to . . .

Since our inception, we have been driven to achieve academic excellence. This is reflected through our programs such as _____, which serve children by . . .

Your child takes part in our _____ program.

Your child attended classes on/in _____ with a specific focus on the skills/topic of . . . this past semester.

The teacher helped students brush up on . . .

Based on my training and educational philosophy, which is aligned with . . . , I feel that . . .

This course will encourage your child to . . .

This class is a mirrored environment designed to serve as a prerequisite to an apprenticeship or career vocation.

The focus has been on . . .

This program serves as a prerequisite to . . .

We have been focusing on major topics such as . . .

Students have been learning about . . . in class.

We have been working with students in the areas of . . .

We have concentrated on . . .

While going to school here, your child has learned . . .

Your child has been taught to . . .

Your child is being instructed in . . . and will upon completion move to . . .

Perfect Phrases to Indicate Compliance with State Guidelines

Parents want to know what you are doing to help students learn. You have to be able to defend what your staff is teaching in the classroom. You also need to align yourself with state curriculum guidelines and district regulations. These materials are not always made available to you, and you may have to seek them out. Every state has a published set of guidelines that you can request, and most can be downloaded online. There is little excuse for a school district or a teacher not to be in compliance with these guidelines. Here are some phrases to show that your curriculum and method of teaching is in compliance:

We are in compliance with . . .

We have complied with both state and federal regulations. Our teachers adhere to strict guidelines that require them to . . .

The curriculum at _____ is designed to mirror state curriculum guidelines.

The _____ statute requires . . . . We are meeting the spirit of this statute by . . .

We are working on a plan of corrective action to ensure our compliance with . . .

We hope to comply with . . . by . . .

We are in the initial phases of compliance and hope to be fully compliant by _____ .

Unorthodox methods of teaching may be acceptable to some, but here at [name institution] we believe in traditional methods that promote . . .

The curriculum dictates . . .

Perfect Phrases for Curriculum Reports

Curriculum reports are generated to show the sequence of material and information being taught to learners. Following are some introductory phrases to use when presenting the curriculum to new faculty members who may want to teach outside of your curriculum framework. When writing up curriculum reports, you may want to remind teachers that the word *curriculum* is used to describe a singular form of study, and that the word *curricula* is used to describe plural forms of study. Curriculum can include, but is not limited to, the production of set courses; the prospectus, program, or syllabus; the core curriculum; and/or the national curriculum within a program of study. Let's start with basic phrases that can be used to introduce materials within a set curriculum. These phrases are written to help you modify how you present the core concepts and can be adapted to meet your school's needs.

_____ is about understanding . . . and the design of curriculum and assessments.

_____ will participate in a unit on . . .

We intend to identify the desired results.

We are choosing to test the merits of . . .

The merits of our claims . . .

We encourage . . . to . . .

To match our learning goals, . . .

We use the appropriate evidence produced by . . .

We like to coach by using the following design: . . .

From the sidelines, our professional staff helps our students . . .

Have no misconceptions about our curriculum design, as it is based upon . . .

Coverage of materials includes . . .

Traditional design is based on . . .

A weaker educational design would be visible if . . .

Our curriculum and assessments grasp the key concepts of . . .

After framing our goals, . . .

We meet specific performance goals.

En route to designing a course curriculum of merit, we have . . .

We are known for taking different approaches to creating courses in order to achieve our identified results.

It is essential that we determine what is or isn't acceptable evidence of academic merit.

Our curriculum teams plan learning experiences and content-based instruction on . . .

Having clear goals has helped us focus on creating courses that pass accreditation standards.

Perspective combined with cutting-edge concepts in higher education has led our institution to . . .

To appropriately meet our standards and assess our goals, we use evidence from assessments and other tools before beginning any plan of action toward the creation of our courses.

We work toward the same content standards when working on curriculum design.

A fair depiction of our curriculum would include, but not be limited to, . . .

Using useful formats and templates, we have created units within our curriculum that allow for . . .

Our curriculum demonstrates established goals.

Basic principles of curriculum design and understanding are evident as a result of . . .

Using assessment evidence, we provide classes that prepare our students for real-world experiences.

The function of our curriculum guide is to serve as a . . .

Varied evidence grounded in performance can transfer between course contents when our departments propose courses to . . .

After the review of curriculum draft designs, . . .

Peer reviews of curriculum are completed in cycles.

The quality of the curriculum as a product is invariably enhanced by . . .

Steadying the influence of variables when creating an academic curriculum can prove challenging.

When applied, the proposed frameworks of the curriculum allow for . . .

Enhanced by cognitive tasks, the curriculum for courses in the _____ department prompts learners to . . .

Referring to curricular models such as . . .

When identifying desired results, our curriculum writers highlight . . .

We use explicit learning experiences and instruction in order to . . .

Design considerations such as . . . are essential in curriculum design.

Some argue backward designs will yield greater coherence and better learning experiences.

Key design questions for curriculum include . . .

National, state, and local standards are always considered when creating curriculum.

Understanding of curriculum design differs depending on . . .

Conceptual uncertainties can arise when designing course curriculum.

Evidence suggests that . . . is the best approach to curriculum design.

After a review of previous courses, we have decided to update the current curriculum in the following ways: . . .

When designing curriculum, it is essential to find meaningful inferences.

Implicating standards that can be understood and used in the classroom for improving comprehension and understanding is essential because . . .

Verifiable claims within a curriculum need to be referenced to build a well-rounded perspective on various issues.

Curriculum theory suggests . . .

Encountering . . . issues in curriculum design is not uncommon.

To over- or underestimate the educational importance of curriculum design would be . . .

Constraints within the curriculum include, but are not limited to, . . .

As we know, a standard is different from a performance indicator; that is why as curriculum writers we create goals and assess evidence by . . .

To gain clarity on our curricular goals, we will need to . . .

When writing long-term goals versus short-term goals, we must refer back to our curriculum and target performance objectives.

Content mastery of curricular materials is an appropriate approach to furthering . . .

Identifying bias within a curriculum serves to . . .

The central purpose of inquiry on why we chose the specific design centers around . . .

Course objectives must mirror the assessment process. Therefore, we ask you to note the following in our curriculum design proposal: . . .

We ask that you refine and resubmit your curriculum proposal for further explanation, as the . . .

Basic terms and core ideas are found within our modular design, which allows our curriculum to be more cohesive in terms of . . .

Universal applications to curriculum design usually include . . .

The curriculum serves as a conceptual lens that learners and instructors can use to provide focus as they further their knowledge about . . .

Content-based curriculum design states . . .

Skill-focused courses rely on concepts developed by . . . designs within a given curriculum.

Framing goals within a curriculum . . .

The minimal requirements for curriculum proposals must include the following details, philosophies, and rationales: . . .

Interpreting curriculum means transforming understanding into . . .

The essential connotations associated with the following curriculum are as follows: . . .

Questioning curriculum design is the fundamental practice of bettering education and learning experiences for students enrolled in our courses, and thus it ultimately helps our learners compete for the best jobs in top markets.

Perfect Phrases for Designing and Assessing Educational Objectives

The following category words can be used if you are giving a talk o
writing statements dealing with the design of educational objective
or assessing the methods to get to the educational objectives. You

can use these words within your phrases to categorize the type of educational objectives you are designing or assessing:

Appropriate contextual knowledge
Categories
Classifications
Generalizations
Knowledge of criteria
Models
Principles
Reliable sources of information
Self-knowledge
Specific details and elements
Strategic knowledge
Structures
Subject-specific skills
Subject-specific techniques
Terminology
Theories
Vocabulary

In your documentation, make sure that you note how objectives will be accomplished by using the verb that best describes the activity. Here is a list of common verbs used in educational objectives:

Absorbing	Classifying
Accounting for	Coaching
Analyzing	Commencing
Applying	Comparing
Ascertaining	Creating
Attributing	Critiquing
Becoming more skilled at	Defending
Checking	Depicting
Clarifying	Differentiating

Discovering	Justifying
Distinguishing	Launching
Edifying	Learning
Educating	Lecturing
Elucidating	Making clear
Engaging	Making students
Engrossing	aware of
Enlightening	Necessitating
Entailing	Occupying
Establishing	Organizing
Evaluating	Planning
Executing	Pointing out
Exemplifying	Portraying
Explaining	Positing
Explicating	Presenting
Expressing	Producing
Familiarizing	Putting into plain words
Finding out about	Rationalizing
Gaining knowledge of	Recalling
Generating	Recognizing
Giving a picture of	Remembering
Giving details for	Requiring
Giving reasons for	Riveting
Grasping	Schooling
Gripping	Showing
Hosting	Starting
Identifying	Studying
Illustrating	Summarizing
Implementing	Taking notes
Inferring	Teaching
Initiating	Telling
Instituting	Training
Instructing	Tutoring
Interpreting	Understanding

In explaining or justifying an educational objective, you will need to show what the objective will enable the learner to do, if accomplished. Explanations may include the following phrases:

Allows the learner to analyze errors

Allows the learner to classify and identify categories

Allows the learner to conduct investigations

Allows the learner to construct symbolic representation

Allows the learner to determine the extent to which he or she can . . .

Allows the learner to establish and identify core beliefs

Allows the learner to execute . . .

Allows the learner to form hypotheses

Allows the learner to identify basic structures of information

Allows the learner to identify errors

Allows the learner to identify logical sequences

Allows the learner to integrate information

Allows the learner to investigate . . .

Allows the learner to make generalizations

Allows the learner to match concepts

Allows the learner to perform a procedure without significant error

Allows the learner to produce . . .

Allows the learner to recall information

Allows the learner to recognize differences

Allows the learner to relate information

Allows the learner to specify . . .

Allows the learner to use information

Some objectives will demonstrate or explain an action to justify the completion of the course or target objective. The following phrases are often used for documentation purposes:

Demonstrates a knowledge of classifications and categories

Demonstrates a knowledge of conventions

Demonstrates a knowledge of methodology

Demonstrates a knowledge of specific facts

Demonstrates a knowledge of terminology

Demonstrates a knowledge of trends or sequences

Demonstrates a level of educational principles

Demonstrates Bloom's taxonomy of evaluation, synthesis, analysis, application, comprehension, and knowledge

Demonstrates educational structures based on accepted theories

Demonstrates educational theories

Demonstrates generalizations in an educational context

Examines process monitoring

Examines student motivation

Examines the efficacy of . . .

Examines the emotional response to . . .

Examines the importance of . . .

In other forms of documentation to justify the learning objective you will need to show the benchmark it meets or the level of ability used. Here are some phrases to help you do this:

Level of processing includes a self-system of evaluation

Level of processing is at analysis

Level of processing is at comprehension

Level of processing is at knowledge utilization

Level of processing is at retrieval

Level of processing uses a metacognitive system

Meets mental procedures

Meets minimum requirements of information required

Meets psychomotor procedures

Evaluating objectives in some documents may require you to phrase your assessments in other ways. Here are some sample phrases to help you with your reports:

Monitors accuracy

Monitors issues in fluency

Objective lets student demonstrate ability to . . .

Offers the learner a chance to experiment with data

Specifies . . . learning goals

Specifies . . . educational objectives

Utilizes important decision-making skills

Utilizes important problem-solving skills

Monitors student's ability to grasp vocabulary terms

Monitors student's ability to grasp facts vs. opinions

Monitors student's ability to grasp time sequences

Monitors student's ability to grasp academic principles

Monitors student's ability to grasp generalizations

Monitors student's ability to grasp concepts of . . .

Encourages students to learn more specific levels of information

Encourages further practice

Looks at categories of mental procedures

Categories of psychomotor procedures

Breaks down the components of the three knowledge domains

Looks at categories of student-related procedures

Addresses the concept of identification

Addresses the issues of similarities and differences

Address the process of . . .

Specifies attributes of . . .

Helps to determine . . .

Identifies defining characteristics

Identifies the analyzing of errors

Looks for patterns or connections

Helps students make general statements

Focuses on specific pieces of information

Identifies the impact of each step

Breaks down learning components by . . .

Corrects faulty or ineffective methods of . . .

Teaches the application of . . .

Helps to identify alternatives

Identifies particular criteria important to . . .

Allows for the selection of alternatives

Allows for systematic application

Allows for the evaluation of alternatives

Allows for the selecting and executing of alternatives

Encourages learners to make predictions

Encourages the design of . . .

Encourages student to work with observational data

Works to identify what is known or agreed upon

Identifies areas of confusion

Provides answers to commonly confused concepts

Monitors accuracy and clarity of specific learning goals

Offers students a self-system of thinking

Determines if a student can examine and differentiate between levels of . . .

Examines importance

Examines efficacy

Examines emotional response to . . .

Examines overall motivation

Allows the individual learner to perceive . . .

Impacts the learning goal by . . .

Retrieves information through recognition

Infers information

Implies inferences and conclusions

Allows for the support of textual evidence with or without prior knowledge

Determines whether incoming information is accurate or inaccurate

Allows student to determine details

Allows students to organize information and ideas

Creates a mental procedure

Creates a structured method for detailing information and organizing ideas

Encourages learners to use list selection

Helps learners to identify from a list

Helps learners to determine if statements are true

Allows for constructed responses

Exemplifies the curriculum frameworks by . . .

When evaluating other objectives, you need to know what the objective is going to allow the learner to do in a specific situation. Here are some sample phrases to help you document:

Lets the learner describe the complex process of . . .

Lets the learner describe how or why . . .

Lets the learner describe cause and effect

Lets the learner describe relationships between . . .

Allows learners to make connections between . . .

Objective depicts . . .

Objective serves to represent . . .

Objective used illustrates . . .

Objective draws upon . . .

Objective is based on the _____ model/theory/ hypotheses

Objective charts student progress by . . .

Sometimes when you are evaluating educational objectives, there is very little leeway because the materials or curriculum to be taught is mandated by the state or the district. In these cases, when evaluating benchmarks, you may want to consider phrasing information as follows:

Requires student to categorize

Requires student to differentiate

Requires student to discriminate

Requires student to distinguish

Requires student to sort

Requires student to create an analogy

Requires students to depict critical elements

Requires students to use like terms

Requires learners to describe critical elements of . . .

The objective requires learners to identify problems

The objective requires learners to identify issues

The objective requires learners to identify misunderstandings between . . .

The objective requires learners to assess and critique . . .

The objective requires learners to diagnose . . .

The objective requires learners to evaluate . . .

The objective requires learners to edit and revise . . .

The objective requires learners to trace the development of . . .

The objective requires learners to draw conclusions

When assessing objectives, you must also apply them to student learning and the students' ability to put the theory into practice. Here are some examples of phrases that describe how the accomplishment of an educational objective affects students:

Begins to track print while listening

Builds a repertoire of spelling words

Can combine information from multiple sources

Can count syllables in a word

Can decode orthographically designed nonsense words

Can discuss similarities and differences

Can incorporate long vocabulary strands

Can name a book title and author

Can present materials to peers

Can rhyme words

Can transition between emergent and real reading

Can write first and last name

Correctly answers comprehension questions

Discusses prior knowledge of topics

Engages in literacy activities

Can differentiate sets of words or shapes

Has a reading vocabulary of _____ sight words

Infers meaning

Knows how to independently review work for . . .

Knows one-to-one letter correspondences

Knows the parts of books and their functions

Listens attentively while the teacher reads in class

Makes reasonable judgments

Monitors behavior during lessons

Notices when simple sentences fail to make sense

Produces a variety of . . . work based on academic materials

Produces a variety of compositions

Productively discusses ways to clarify information

Reads aloud with accuracy

Reads familiar texts or words

Recalls facts and details of texts

Recognizes irregularly spelled words

Recognizes letters in upper and lowercase

Rereads information

Retells stories with accuracy

Shows evidence of expanding language

Understands how to manipulate responses

Understands the content of materials studied

Uses basic punctuation and spelling

Uses critical thinking skills

Uses how, why, and what-if questions

Uses knowledge to print sound mappings

With some guidance, can produce . . .

Writes to express his or her own meaning

To put an educational objective on a paper is not enough. More concrete information must follow the objective in the documentation such as the methods used. Here are some topical words that may jog your mind when wording other sections of the document:

Appreciation	Knowledge
Attitudes and opinions	Recitation
Behavior	Skills
Concomitant	Subject matter
Habits	Thinking ability

When you want to explain ways that students will acquire information through educational objectives, you may want to use these types of phrases:

Talking with others

Expressing experiences

Acquiring reading habits

Attending lectures

Developing thinking habits in learning how to attack problems

Experimenting

Conducting investigations

Making observations

Exercising intellect

Making progress charts

Following health regimes

Playing games

Engaging in debates

Attending concerts

Keeping scrapbooks

Doing artwork

Making descriptive and analytic drawings and diagrams

We are using the following assessment to measure . . .

Chapter 7

Other Important Phrases for Administrators

This chapter contains a collection of phrases for a variety of situations and purposes that can prove invaluable for administrators.

Perfect Phrases for Defining a School Within a District

In a single district, regular public schools, trade schools, charter schools, safe school programs, magnet schools, and alternative schools can all be managed under one superintendent. Some districts have separate superintendents for different types of schools. For example, there may be a superintendent of the middle and high schools and a different superintendent for the elementary school. In other districts, there may be a superintendent for the academic schools and a separate superintendent for the vocational schools. Some schools can be defined by the programs that are offered to their learners. More charter schools for intensive language training, the arts, and technology have become noticeable in districts. Educational administrators promote the diverse programs in these schools to entice more students to stay in school to lower dropout rates.

If you are a new school administrator, you will soon learn that schools within a district are constrained by financial budgets. This is a fact that experienced superintendents and principals know all too well. Schools are budgeted certain amounts of money based on the number of students attending their programs. And with school choice programs, some districts have to pay money out to other districts for students who don't want to attend their local town or city schools. This is why promoting a public education to elementary, middle, or high school parents has become commonplace, especially within varying school systems. Many people are under the mistaken assumption only the private or parochial school districts are looking for prospective students for future classes. These educational leaders must sell their programs in order to justify tuition rates, but public school administrators have similar issues because for every student they lose from a district, money is lost from the budget. So school districts have to work on the same premise as private and parochial schools in many instances.

As the administrator of a school or program, you will need to meet with incoming students' parents to sell your school and its programs. During the presentation, you want to sell and market your school by highlighting its programs in order to attract the students to your school. In many cases, once students come to a school, even if they drop out or attend another school in the district, you can keep the money allotted for them in your budget. It is in your best interest to show quality programs at the most affordable price in the safest learning conditions. This section offers phrases that can be used to demonstrate competitive programs and/or to introduce your school to the general public.

We are on the cutting edge in the areas of . . .

Your child's education and safety are our top priority.

We stand above the other institutions because we . . .

We are one of the first to . . .

Our reputation for quality has withstood the test of time since . . .

We are ranked among . . . as one of the top . . .

We offer the finest traditions due to our merit and award-winning teachers.

We offer the best quality education for price in these difficult economic times.

We offer _____ in scholarships to our students.

Our students have gone on to become . . .

Our prestigious alumni include . . .

Our splendid record of great achievement consists of . . .

We have a low student-to-teacher ratio.

The percentage of our students who make or exceed state averages is . . .

We encourage active parental involvement.

Perfect Phrases for Writing School Grants

In any organization, including schools, a good grant writer can more than fund his or her own salary. Asking teachers to write grants is another option, but with their workloads, it is nearly impossible for them to meet the requirements effectively. As an educational leader, learning to write grants is essential. It is important work, and if you know how to do it you can bring money into your school district. Following are recommended steps in writing a grant proposal or responding to a request for response (RFR).

The first thing to do is to read the grant to make sure your school or district is a match. If the grant says your school must have a high population of Sudanese students to qualify, and you write it for a school made up primarily of Hispanics, then you have wasted your time and probably eliminated your chances of winning the grant.

Second, you must compose an inquiry letter. An inquiry letter should be worded something like the following:

July 13, 2010

Douglas Wilson, Grant Chairperson
Kilmarnoch Park Cottage Foundation
303 Muirhouse Road
Pittsfield, NY 35217

Re: Letter of Inquiry

Dear Mr. Wilson,

Thank you for our recent meeting at the Kilmarnoch Park Cottage Foundation (KPCF) where you were kind enough to offer us a follow-up visit with our staff. We appreciated the time you took to learn about our mission and current projects. We thoroughly enjoyed your visit with us, and we sincerely appreciate your thoughtful attention to our ESOL program for refugee students attending New York public schools.

Your interest in our refugee students from Central Asia and the Middle East is a significant acknowledgment of our successful track record of delivering superior education projects to school-age refugees for nearly thirty-four years.

We are aware that the KPCF distributes a number of grants for educational purposes. We wish to apply for one of the Foundation's grants.

I am pleased to write to you about a project that I believe will be of interest to the KPFC. We are seeking $50,000 over three years to expand our very successful language education program to provide aggressive, hands-on intensive English language training to refugee students living in new communities around the greater upstate New York area.

We are also seeking support from the Foundation to enable us to develop a pilot for an ESOL program for war refugee children with strict Islamic backgrounds. We ask for your partnership because of the Foundation's demonstrated interest in alternative education, especially for those from the underrepresented minority communities. We critically need funds to launch this sorely needed language training program and to fund equipment, software, and the resources of two teachers to oversee and assist the volunteer student educators from Crane College. These equipment and support resources will constructively assist the two hundred undereducated minority residents to be served by our new community ESL language program. The ethnic composition is approximately 49 percent Iraqi, 26 percent Palestinian, 9 percent Uzbek, 9 percent Yemeni, and 7 percent Algerian. We look forward to hearing positively from your organization in the near future.

Sincerely,

*Katherine Sarah-Eileen Wilson and
Alexander John Patrick Wilson*

Executive Director and Principal Language Educator

Attachments: audited financial statement for the most recent fiscal year, current IRS 501(c)(3) designation, and annual report

Upon completion of your inquiry letter comes the real workload, and this is why grant money doesn't come flowing into schools. The grant application documents can sometimes look like a Greek translation of legalese. After reading through the grant information, grant writers must attempt to figure out what they are being asked to write and the expectations of the grant organization. With few volunteers willing to do the paperwork, coupled with the fact that school grant announcements come at the busiest time of the school year, many grants proposals don't get written and a lot of money isn't used.

But with a little preparation and some good phrases, you can write a proper grant proposal to earn money for your school projects. The first step is developing a one-page school summary. The summary page should have information that reads almost like a checklist. For school grants the summary page should include such items as the project's name; submission due date and time; and mailing address to submit the application for the grant. The grant itself will tell you all the pertinent information, such as the prior notification date and contact; number of copies required; preferred font, margins, and spacing; page limit and location of page numbers; and preferences and eligibility requirements. Before embarking on this endeavor, make sure to read and reread the restrictions on grant money use, goals of the funding, acceptable uses of grant money, and requirements for signatures and assurances.

Follow the grant sentence by sentence. A solid piece of advice is to answer what the grant asks for, instead of injecting what you think the grant organization needs to hear. In most instances, don't include pictures or other information that isn't relevant. Often those who just follow the directions are awarded grants, because they show that the school understands the spirit of the grant.

When writing any grant proposal for your school, you must introduce your connection to the purpose for which the money is intended and your need for the proposed project. If your school is a religious private school, you may not be eligible for some government-funded grants. There may not be a connection to justify why government money should fund a religious-based program. But you can word grants in odd situations to fit your district's needs. Let's look at this sample:

The problems at Hinsdale High School, whose ten-room building is settled in the Appalachian mountains of the United States, are common to many rural areas across the western end of Massachusetts. Issues faced by our central Berkshire school include (1) student isolation from cultural activities, (2) increasing numbers of at-risk families, (3) increasing risk of juvenile alcohol/tobacco/drug use, (4) increasing numbers of students at risk for academic failure, (5) low per-pupil expenditures, and (6) high teenage pregnancy rates coupled with high dropout rates.

When writing the grant, you may want to incorporate phrases that show you will meet national and state standards. In these situations, you may want to phrase your wording in the grant like the following example:

All food facilities used in the hunger project are accessible and meet federal standards. The Ashford youth program will be providing food during the before and after school programs in three ways: (1) through federal after-school nutrition subsidies, (2) through donations from local businesses, and (3) from surplus vendor samples.

When writing the grant, you will need to create charts that show goals, aims, and objectives with quantitative data. These goals should have measurable outcomes. The measurable outcomes can be submitted in chart form to demonstrate the program components, activities, outcomes, and measurable indicators.

You will need a framework and a timeline to demonstrate how you will complete these objectives, as well as a budget showing required expenditures.

You may have to demonstrate the process by which each goal will be met by using phrases such as the following:

In Phase 1 of Washington-Carver District's plan, the Kandiko Computer Aided Language Learning Project intends to bring Arabic language to rural towns. It will consist of five steps: (1) data collection by language type, (2) data entry by language progress, (3) computer-based storage of syntactical differences, (4) computer-based statistical analysis, and (5) reporting to measure if the English speakers were able to acquire a second language in an intensive program meeting for a set number of mornings under the direction of a native speaker.

If you want a grant awarded to your school, as the administrator, you will need to demonstrate how you will collect data, maintain grant records, and sustain the program once the grant has ended.

The grant writer should for safety purposes write a basic conclusion rephrasing what the grant or RFR asked for in its proposal, inserting your school's information in the appropriate places.

Perfect Phrases for Professional Development

Teachers either like or dislike professional development (PD). Teachers who like professional development will always be in attendance. This section is written for the educator or administrator who has to coax unwilling teachers to a professional development event. Some states have started to make professional development mandatory for license renewal. The following phrases can help administrators promote programs for teacher development to encourage educators to show up and actively participate.

This program will enhance your professional growth.

Change is inevitable. This professional development workshop will challenge you to . . .

In the spirit of . . . , the district will offer professional development workshops for . . .

Productive faculty members are seen as those who show initiative to attend PD programs.

Possibilities are endless when you learn something new. Come to our PD event!

Potential knowledge coupled with education means success! Join us for the workshop on . . .

Transform your favorite teaching lesson into a sharing session for colleagues. Attend our lesson swap shop session for teacher professional development!

In order to fulfill requirements for . . . , teachers are expected to attend _____ professional development sessions.

Teacher Enrichment Program Opportunity: [list workshop/ date/time]

Become proficient in . . . at our teacher PD workshop session.

Master new skills at the PD session offered . . . for . . .

First-rate speakers will be training teachers in the areas of . . .

Motivated teachers wanted to attend a dynamic presentation on . . .

Perfect Phrases for Faculty Notices

Keep statements simple and factual in faculty notices. As an administrator, it is a good idea never to explain the reasoning behind a statement in a faculty notice because it gives disgruntled staff members something to pick away at or to complain about later with other teachers. These notices are not personal statements, but rather neutral comments that provide information. Following are some handy phrases associated with faculty notices that will prove helpful.

A student will be removed from an uncomfortable situation if . . .

Emergency lockdown is required if . . .

Evaluation services are offered to students.

Fire and emergency drills will take place . . .

Food and drink are prohibited in the classroom.

In an emergency, exit the building using the nearest open door.

In case of an evacuation, students and faculty are asked to . . .

In order to evaluate performance, students will be asked to . . .

In order to expedite the process, . . .

In order to extract the data, each child will need . . .

It has been established that . . .

It is estimated that . . .

It is important to edit documents before sending them out to the general public.

It is necessary to exert all necessary precautions.

Our system has not failed us in the past.

Please examine all copies.

Students must enter the schools through designated areas, which are marked by clear signs on the walls.

Students showing signs of underperformance will be required to . . .

Students who are expelled are responsible for . . .

If a child becomes uncontrollable in your classroom, district policy states . . .

Students will be evaluated on . . .

Teachers are not permitted to hand out any drugs or medication to students.

The principal has asked our student body to participate in . . .

Unapproved electrical devices may not be used in the classroom.

Study hall teachers should report to room _____ .

Perfect Phrases for Student Bulletins

When you think back to your school days, you probably remember your teachers far more than your administration. How the administrators worded information they relayed determined the "information" that you knew. Not all information for students needs to be announced over the intercom, however. Many teachers prefer a written bulletin that they can post for students to read. First, a written bulletin is appreciated by instructors because it is less of a distraction, and second, it can list repeated facts that are used to remind students of information from guidance and administrators. The bulletin can be broken into sections. The student academic section should have a separate space in the bulletin for sports announcements.

The lunch menu for the week will be . . .

Scholarship forms are now available in the guidance office.

The library will be closed tomorrow.

There will be a meeting for all Cub Scouts after school with Mr. Plumb in the cafeteria.

Students are reminded that all class dues must be paid in full by _____ .

Perfect Phrases for Student Announcements

The daily announcements over the intercom system should include information and reminders about current school activities and events, as well as important reminders about school policies or procedures. Listed are sample announcements for all students:

Students are offered student counseling by peer resources/ professionals/volunteers.

Students can be recommended for the _____ award. If you feel that a student is deserving, you may nominate him or her by . . .

Students' artwork has been displayed in . . .

Students are reminded that . . .

The magazine drive kickoff date will be _____. See your homeroom teacher for details.

All students interested in the trip to the United Arab Emirates should report to room _____ and sign up with Mr. Ibrahim.

Kat Wilson will be offering a free lecture on _____ to all students at the Lanesboro Public Library on _____ at _____. Anyone interested in attending should pick up a permission slip from Mr. Alex no later than at the end of lunch today.

There will be a general assembly on Monday afternoon. All students should report to the auditorium at _____.

All students and teachers will be processed for IDs on _____.

School pictures will be taken on _____ during school hours. Students are reminded that payment is due at that time. Retakes will be made available to students on _____.

There will be no school on Friday due to in-service workshops for teachers.

All staff and students are reminded to remove all metal objects before going through the security detectors.

Reminder to all students: unless you have a written note from . . . , you may not ride any school bus other than your designated bus.

The Regents Exams are scheduled for next week. Teachers are asked not to assign homework on test days.

Teachers are reminded to post the daily bulletin for students to read.

The Right Phrase for
Every Situation...Every Time

Perfect Phrases for Building Strong Teams
Perfect Phrases for Business Letters
Perfect Phrases for Business Proposals and Business Plans
Perfect Phrases for Business School Acceptance
Perfect Phrases for College Application Essays
Perfect Phrases for Cover Letters
Perfect Phrases for Customer Service
Perfect Phrases for Dealing with Difficult People
Perfect Phrases for Dealing with Difficult Situations at Work
Perfect Phrases for Documenting Employee Performance Problems
Perfect Phrases for Executive Presentations
Perfect Phrases for Landlords and Property Managers
Perfect Phrases for Law School Acceptance
Perfect Phrases for Lead Generation
Perfect Phrases for Managers and Supervisors
Perfect Phrases for Managing Your Small Business
Perfect Phrases for Medical School Acceptance
Perfect Phrases for Meetings
Perfect Phrases for Motivating and Rewarding Employees
Perfect Phrases for Negotiating Salary & Job Offers
Perfect Phrases for Perfect Hiring
Perfect Phrases for the Perfect Interview
Perfect Phrases for Performance Reviews
Perfect Phrases for Real Estate Agents & Brokers
Perfect Phrases for Resumes
Perfect Phrases for Sales and Marketing Copy
Perfect Phrases for the Sales Call
Perfect Phrases for Setting Performance Goals
Perfect Phrases for Small Business Owners
Perfect Phrases for the TOEFL Speaking and Writing Sections
Perfect Phrases for Writing Grant Proposals
Perfect Phrases in American Sign Language for Beginners
Perfect Phrases in French for Confident Travel
Perfect Phrases in German for Confident Travel
Perfect Phrases in Italian for Confident Travel
Perfect Phrases in Spanish for Confident Travel to Mexico
Perfect Phrases in Spanish for Construction
Perfect Phrases in Spanish for Gardening and Landscaping
Perfect Phrases in Spanish for Household Maintenance and Child Care
Perfect Phrases in Spanish for Restaurant and Hotel Industries

Visit mhprofessional.com/perfectphrases for a complete product listing.

Learn more. Mc Graw Hill Do more.

CPSIA information can be obtained
at www.ICGtesting.com
Printed in the USA
FFOW03n2328080715
14954FF